WHY WON'T
MEN ASK FOR
DIRECTIONS?

WHY WON'T MEN ASK FOR DIRECTIONS?

APANDISIS
α
PUBLISHING

Apandisis Publishing
105 Madison Avenue, Suite 3A
New York, New York 10016

ISBN-13: 978-1-4127-5277-0
ISBN-10: 1-4127-5277-9

Manufactured in USA

8 7 6 5 4 3 2 1

www.FYIanswers.com

Contents

Chapter Three
TRADITIONS

Chapter Four
LOVE AND LUST

Chapter Five
ANIMAL KINGDOM

Chapter Six
SPORTS

Chapter Seven
FOOD AND DRINK

Chapter Eight
EARTH AND SPACE

Chapter Nine
HISTORY

Chapter Ten
WEIRD SCIENCE AND TECHNOLOGY

Chapter Eleven
ORIGINS

Chapter Twelve
BODY SCIENCE

Chapter Thirteen
MORE GOOD STUFF

Chapter One

PEOPLE

Q Why won't men ask for directions?

A Everyone's heard the old joke that asks, "Why does it take one hundred million sperm to fertilize one egg?" Answer: "Because none of them will stop for directions."

The stereotype that men refuse to ask for directions has been fertile territory for amateur comedians over the years; at the same time, experience seems to suggest that there may be some truth to it. In fact, we suspect that plenty of women—perhaps one reading this right now, as she is being driven farther and farther away from her destination by a man who insists he is not lost—are eagerly awaiting the answer to this question.

Though it might be small consolation, researchers have claimed to have evidence suggesting that men's disinclination to ask for directions may be because they have a better chance of not getting lost in the first place. According to a 2000 study in *Nature Neuroscience*, men might have trouble asking for directions simply because they are naturally better than women at finding their way around. The study, which examined men's and women's brain responses to spatial puzzles, found that the left hippocampal region—the part of the brain involved in spatial problems—activated more frequently and intensely in men than in women. Accordingly, men were consistently better than women at solving spatial and directional puzzles. The study posits that men use more geometric or spatial cues to get around, while women tend to use landmarks. (This helps explain why women more frequently say, "Go left at the McDonald's," while men tend to say, "Head east on Main Street" when providing directions.)

How did this develop? For the answer, we look to socio-biologists, evolutionary experts who attempt to explain biological traits based on evolutionary theory; in particular, natural selection. According to socio-biologists, men developed better neural compasses because way back in their chest-beating, club-wielding caveman days, males foraged far and wide for food for their families, while females stayed in the caves, tending to the youngsters. Better foragers—with better senses of direction—not only had increased chances of survival, but also proved more attractive as potential mates; thus, the genes for "direction" were passed on.

So, ladies, the next time you find yourself cruising in the middle of nowhere for several hours while your husband claims that he's not lost, give him a break. There's a good chance that he just can't help it. Now, if only those socio-biologists could figure out why men can't put the toilet seat down or throw their dirty clothes into the hamper.

Q Do prisoners still make license plates?

A If you live and drive in the United States, there's a good chance that your car's license plate was made by prison inmates. Forty-seven states, plus the District of Columbia, rely on correctional facilities to manufacture license plates. Only Alaska, Hawaii, and Oregon do not utilize convict labor.

License plates date nearly to the dawn of the automobile. New York was the first state to require them, in 1901, and others soon followed. Each car was assigned a number, and its owner was expected to make the license plate. Not surprisingly, this led to a variety of strange and interesting designs. Most plates were fashioned from wood, leather, or porcelain. For years, Sears, Roebuck and Co. offered a license-plate design kit in its mail-order catalog. Massachusetts began issuing standardized plates in 1903, and within fifteen years, every state had followed suit.

The link between prisons and plates has its roots in a movement in the late nineteen hundreds toward more benevolent treatment of the incarcerated. It produced reforms that mandated inmates be given useful, productive work.

Pennsylvania was the first state to have prisoners make license plates. In 1920, John R. Wald, superintendent of the state's Prison Labor Division, invented a die machine for stamping letters and numbers on metal plates. He installed it in the Huntington Reformatory; by 1924, Huntington inmates were producing eleven thousand license plates a day. Other state prison systems quickly instituted similar programs.

Plate-making prisoners have adapted to new technology over the years. The Digital License Plate system, developed by technology giant 3M, enables individuals and groups to develop custom license-plate designs on a computer. Prison officials initially feared the software would put them out of the license-plate business, but inmates proved to be adept with the high-tech tools. Some states take orders for plates from all over the world.

Inmates today make everything from sneakers to circuit boards. Some work as call-center representatives, filling merchandise orders and booking hotel rooms. But regardless of whatever else they do, prisoners will always be best known for license plates. And for many of these inmates, the license plates that they produce are their only connections to the glorious freedom of the open road.

Q Can a woman be a nun if she's not a virgin?

A You can be a nun without your virginity—whether you lost it casually as a young person or on your wedding night. You can even be a nun if you have children. The list of requirements to become a nun is amazingly small. As wisegeek.com puts it, "One must be Catholic, female, unmarried, and sane."

Religious orders are considerably more uptight about divorce than virginity; divorce is generally the biggest sticking point to joining the sisterhood. A divorced woman who wants to be a nun has to have the marriage annulled by the church, and this requires proving that the marriage was somehow invalid or entered into under false pretenses.

A woman who wants to enter a religious order must merely demonstrate that she is mature, in control of her emotions and herself, and prepared for a life of celibacy. There is, of course, some fine print. For example, a woman who has children who are under the ages of eighteen typically can't become a nun because the sisterhood requires devotion to a prayerful life that doesn't leave enough time for parenting.

If you're surprised by the relative liberalism of the rules, consider as well that if a novice (as a nun-in-training is called) decides that the nun's life is not for her, religious orders are generally understanding of her choice. But after the several-year training process is completed, a change of heart is strongly frowned upon.

Even with a bunch of one-night stands in your past, you can get into the sisterhood fairly easily. It's the getting out part that raises eyebrows.

Q Are attractive people more successful?

A Brace yourself, especially if you're a woman sporting a five o'clock shadow or a man with a hunchback. The news isn't good: Attractive people are richer and more successful than the rest of us.

So say University of California researchers who sought to discover whether there's a beauty bias in the workplace. Reporting in the *Journal of Economic Psychology,* they found that the prettiest people make 12 percent more money than their less-comely counterparts. The main reason: It's much easier for attractive people to generate cooperation among co-workers.

"Controlled studies show people go out of their way to help attractive people—of the same and opposite sex—because they want to be liked and accepted by good-looking people," says Dr. Gordon Patzer, a researcher who's addressed this phenomenon for more than thirty years. Hiring managers and HR professionals may deny any link between workforce favoritism and physical beauty, but researchers maintain that the beauty bias exists in all occupations.

It was found in the field of law by economics professors Daniel Hamermesh of the University of Texas and Jeff Biddle of Michigan State University. Their report, "Beauty, Productivity and Discrimination: Lawyers' Looks and Lucre," revealed that the chances of a male attorney getting an early partnership are linked to his attractiveness. Who says justice is blind?

Researcher Patzer says this type of bias is genetic: We're set up to react positively to the beauty and negatively to the beast. And that can influence success.

"Good looks have what social scientists call the *halo effect,*" explains Catherine Kaputa, a work strategist and the author of *U R a*

Brand! How Smart People Brand Themselves for Business Success. "Because someone is attractive, we assign many other positive attributes to him or her that have nothing to do with looks."

Who knew work was a bona fide beauty contest? Want to get ahead? Better get a makeover.

Q Do important people still have food tasters?

A In the days of yore, kings and emperors were especially wary of being offed by rivals. A popular method of offing was poisoning the intended victim's food. So when an elite was about to eat, it was a food taster's job to test the meal for dangerous substances.

The test was simple. If a taster fell ill after sampling the roast beef, His Majesty would wisely opt for the fish. A corollary benefit of this arrangement was protection against non-intentional poisoning. In an era when bloodletting was considered an advanced medical treatment, food storage and preparation standards were not quite as stringent as they are today. If you could afford such a luxury, it was a fine idea to have somebody who was expendable to enjoy a taste before you sat down to eat.

Today, security professionals envelop world leaders, and food sanitation is vastly improved. You might think, then, that the job of the food taster has gone the way of the alchemist, but the people who guard the president of the United States do include culinary concerns among their responsibilities.

Details of modern food-tasting security are sketchy—keeping secrets is a big part of security, after all—but a 2005 book, *Standing Next to History: An Agent's Life Inside the Secret Service*, provides a glimpse into today's culinary clandestineness. Author and former Secret Service agent Joseph Petro says that when the president eats at an official dinner overseas or anywhere outside the White House, the dish is the same as everyone else's. The president's meal, however, is prepared from ingredients delivered and prepared separately by vetted staff. Even the server who hands the meal to the president is assigned the job by the security corps.

When taste testers are used for important people, they might not be human. At the 2008 Olympic Games in Beijing, samples of food being prepared for athletes were fed to white mice. These mice generally show the effects of tainted or poisoned food within about seventeen hours, a shorter period than it would take to produce lab results.

Hey, whatever works. But back in the day, the queen would probably have fainted if vermin had been involved in the preparation of her feast.

Q Why does the pope change his name when he takes office?

A Think of it as a safety measure to ensure that the papacy remains classy. The tradition started in the year 533: The Catholic Church had just selected a new pope whose given name was Mercurius, a reference to Mercury, the Roman god of commerce. After centuries of stamping out paganism, having a pope named after a pagan god wouldn't do. So Mercurius became John II.

Over the next several centuries, a few other popes changed their names, but these were exceptions rather than the rule. It wasn't until the year 1009 that name changing became the "in" thing. That's when a pope was chosen who had an unfortunate name: Pietro Osporci. His first name just wouldn't work, since it was derived from Saint Peter, Prince of Apostles and Pontiff *Numero Uno*. (No pope has ever taken this name, because none would compare himself to Saint Peter.) Even worse, Osporci means "pig's snout," so that was no good, either. He chose a more dignified moniker, Sergius IV, and changing names was established as a standard practice. Since then, only two popes—Hadrian VI and Marcellus II, both in the sixteenth century—have kept their birth names.

The practice of taking on a new name can have a spiritual dimension as well. In the Old Testament, for example, an angel defeats Jacob in a wrestling match, demonstrating the sovereignty of God; he then gives Jacob the name Israel, meaning "God commands." And the New Testament tells the story of a man named Simon whom Jesus renamed Peter (and who eventually became Saint Peter) when he became a disciple. In this way, a name change can signify the beginning of a new spiritual life, often in an elevated position.

And what position could be more elevated than the pope's? This may be why renaming is one of the first orders of business after a new pope is selected. As soon as the elected pope accepts the position, the Dean of the College of Cardinals asks him, *"Quomodo vis vocari?"* ("By what name do you wish to be called?")

There's no *Big Book of Pope Names* to consult, but new popes generally name themselves after their predecessors or saints they hope to emulate. For example, the current pope said this about his choice of Benedict XVI: "Firstly, I remember Pope Benedict XV, that courageous prophet of peace, who guided the Church through turbulent times of war. In his footsteps, I place my ministry in the service of reconciliation and harmony between peoples. Additionally, I recall Saint Benedict of Nursia, co-patron of Europe, whose life evokes the Christian roots of Europe. I ask him to help us all to hold firm to the centrality of Christ in our Christian life: May Christ always take first place in our thoughts and actions."

The name may not be as cool as Pope Awesome the First, but it has a nice ring to it.

Q Who lives at the ends of the earth?

A Throughout history, people from every culture and walk of life have conjured images of far-off, mythical places with exotic names like Xanadu, Shangri-La, and Milwaukee.

This universal desire to fantasize about unknown lands likely gave rise to such terms as "the four corners of the earth" and "the ends of the earth." These phrases suggest that somewhere on our plane of existence exist identifiable, ultimate nether regions—locations farther away from us than any other. A search of the King James Bible turns up no fewer than twenty-eight occurrences of the term "ends of the earth." Psalm 72:8, for example, reads,

"He shall have dominion also from sea to sea, and from the river unto the ends of the earth." This is a translation of the Latin *Et dominabitur a mari usque ad mare, et a flumine usque ad terminos terrae.* At a time when guys in togas and sandals went around speaking to each other in Latin, most folks probably did believe that the earth was flat and really did have ends.

Today, most of us don't use the term so literally. It's relative and open to your imagination. The ends of the earth could mean the North Pole. If you live in Paris or Rome, perhaps it means the remote Amazon jungle. And if you live on a Himalayan peak, maybe it means Milwaukee.

Q Can it be over before the fat lady sings?

A Yogi Berra, the Hall of Fame catcher for the New York Yankees, was as famous for his verbal foibles as for his baseball skills. Yogi on memory: "This is like *deja vu* all over again." On economics: "A nickel isn't worth a dime today." On making tough choices: "When you come to a fork in the road, take it."

"It ain't over until the fat lady sings" sounds like it would be a Yogism, especially since he coined this similar gem: "It ain't over till it's over." But this isn't the case. "It ain't over until the fat lady sings" made its way into popular usage in the 1970s. Though it's most often called upon to describe sporting events, this pearl of wisdom has also been applied to other forms of competition— like when a beaming Bill Clinton showed up to a 1992 election party in Arkansas wearing a T-shirt that sported the phrase "The Fat Lady Sang." (Knowing William Jefferson Clinton's reputation, onlookers would've been excused for wondering whether or not the phrase really was just a figure of speech.)

But even though the term is a recent creation, pinpointing its origin is surprisingly difficult. The *Washington Post* has suggested one theory, attributing the saying to a San Antonio sportswriter by the name of Dan Cook. According to the *Post,* it was overheard and picked up by Dick Motta, then the coach of the Washington Bullets, who used it through-out the Bullets' 1978 run to the NBA champion-ship. (The fat lady sang for the Bullets in 1997, when their name was changed to the Wiz-ards.)

The second (and less likely) theory refers to the American singer Kate Smith, a portly soprano who reached prominence in the 1930s and 1940s. Ms. Smith—known to Yankees fans today as the voice singing "God Bless America" during the seventh-inning stretch—was in great demand at ribbon-cutting ceremo-nies, political conventions, World Series games, and the like, often closing these events with her version of the Irving Berlin standard. Is Smith the "fat lady"? It's an intriguing possibility, but it's pretty unlikely. For one, she didn't *always* cap her appear-ances with "God Bless America."

Regardless of its origin, the phrase now evokes an image of the opera—or at least a caricature of that pompous art form. Ameri-

can sports fans don't exactly have a reputation for being cultur-
ally sophisticated; the closest some of them get to the art world
is painting their faces before the big game. When they think of
opera, they envision an enormous woman, usually wearing a
horned helmet, belting out the final notes before the curtain falls.

This image—probably drawn from the character of Brünnhilde
in Wagner's *Ring Cycle*—has become shorthand for opera in the
non-opera world. And even though Wagner's opera might not
end until the fat lady sings, the curtain falls for most of us well
before then. That's because we fall asleep sometime during the
first act.

Q Are first-borns more successful?

A This one gets dicey because there are so many different
definitions of success. Nevertheless, the evidence shows that
first-borns are higher achievers according to some conventional
metrics, like school performance and earning power.

According to Michael Grose, author of the book *Why First-Borns
Rule the World and Why Last-Borns Want To Change It,* every
U.S. astronaut from the inception of the space program until
2003 was a first-born. More than half of U.S. presidents have
been first-borns, as have most Nobel Prize winners. First-borns
are also more likely to be entrepreneurs. You get the pattern.

But why? Maybe it comes down to superior brainpower, as those
know-it-all first-borns have been claiming all along. First-borns

do tend to have slightly higher IQs than their siblings—about three points higher on average—according to the results of a study published in 2007 in the journals *Science* and *Intelligence*. This may be because of the undivided attention first-borns receive from their parents during infancy, when cognitive function develops most rapidly. Or it may be because of the challenging roles that first-borns often play in the household, such as mentoring their younger siblings. It may even be because of physical differences owing entirely to birth order.

Evidence points more to nurture than to nature. The 2007 study noted that kids who became the eldest after the death of an older sibling scored like biological first-borns. Still, scientists are intrigued by the apparent influence of birth order on physical development. First-borns, for example, tend to suffer more from asthma than their younger siblings.

Even if first-borns are more successful by our conventional measurements, there's reason for younger siblings to take heart. It's been noted that later-borns tend to find unconventional success that can be both dramatic and enduring. Charles Darwin, Nicolaus Copernicus, and Descartes each had at least two older siblings. As one expert put it, it's the difference between "innovation and radical innovation." Apparently, it takes all kinds.

Q Was Saint Patrick a drunk?

A Before being beatified and canonized, Saint Patrick was a shepherd, a priest, and then a bishop. Though he famously established the shamrock as Ireland's national symbol, his greatest accomplishment was bringing Christianity to those unrepentant pagans of the Emerald Isle. Given his ecclesiastical importance, one has to ask: How in heaven has a holiday named after this pious man turned into the most prodigious drinking day of the year?

Saint Patrick's Day is on March 17, which is also known as the Feast of Saint Patrick. "Feast"—a word occasionally connoting gluttonous celebration—would seem to provide a clue as to why Saint Patrick's Day has become synonymous with watching some amateur blow chunks into a green bowler hat at two in the afternoon, but the truth is that *all* saints have feast days. And when was the last time you saw drink specials being advertised at your local pub for Saint George's Day?

Although it would be all too easy to blame this drunken turn on the fabled alcohol consumption of the Irish, that's another red herring—Saint Patrick's Day was, until recently, celebrated strictly as a religious holiday in Ireland. It wasn't until 1996, when the government of Ireland began a multi-day Saint Patrick's Day Festival, that the Irish iteration of the holiday took on some of the revelrous trappings that are common to the celebration in North America, like a big-time parade.

In fact, parades—specifically, a proliferation of parades—may help explain the roots of North America's drunk-a-thon version of Saint Patrick's Day. The first recorded colonial celebration of Saint Patrick's Day was in Boston in 1737. Not to be outdone, New York City held its own celebration in 1756; its first parade marched into history in 1762. In 1824, parade traditions commenced in Savannah, Georgia, and Montreal. Before long,

Chicago was dying its river green and people from seemingly every other town and city in North America were celebrating Saint Patrick's Day with ale-soaked antics. Because, after all, what else are you going to do while you wait for the parade to start?

Through all of this contagious partying, Saint Patrick's Day has evolved into a holiday that is more secular than religious in nature. It's essentially about good times. You certainly don't have to be Irish to raise a glass (or nine) in honor of Saint Patrick. Whoever he was.

Q Whatever happened to Bat Boy?

A As a *Weekly World News* headline might have read: BAT BOY LIVES! Launched in 1979, *Weekly World News* was a compilation of weird stories from legitimate papers that were sensationalized for maximum effect. But when the editors couldn't round up enough good material, they filled the rest of the issue with fabricated tales of aliens, Bigfoot, and anything else they could dream up.

Eventually, *WWN* began to fabricate the majority of its stories. Avidly read by true believers and others who appreciated the outrageous and often amusing content, the tabloid was a rousing success. At its peak in the late 1980s, *WWN*, produced by a small staff with minimal expenses, had a circulation of 1.2 million.

In 1992, *WWN* struck a chord with the tale of Bat Boy, a half-boy, half-bat who was discovered in a West Virginia cave. The Bat

Boy issue—featuring a freakish, clearly fake picture of a boy with pointy ears, sharp teeth, and huge eyes—flew off the shelves. Many more Bat Boy stories followed, and the creature became the magazine's unofficial mascot.

Many of the stories described Bat Boy's exploits as he craftily eluded police and scientists; he also periodically endorsed presidential candidates and once ran for governor of California. In 2003, he led police in a high-speed chase while driving a Mini Cooper—a cover story that was actually part of a Mini Cooper ad campaign. *WWN* also published a Bat Boy comic strip in 2004, chronicling the creature's rise to the position of president of the United States, among other things. Bat Boy even inspired *Bat Boy: The Musical,* a critically acclaimed, award-winning stage production that debuted in 1997.

In 2007, Bat Boy and the rest of *WWN*'s characters had a near-death experience. With circulation at less than ninety thousand, the tabloid's owner, American Media, ceased publication of the print edition. When the final issue came out in August 2007, it appeared that Bat Boy's adventures had come to an end.

But in October 2008, an enterprising entertainment executive named Neil McGinness bought *WWN* and formed a new company: Bat Boy, LLC. McGinness revamped the *WWN* Web site and started working on merchandising deals, including Bat Boy calendars and toys. Bat Boy's autobiography, *The Audacity of Sonar,* was also put in the works, and McGinness considered relaunching the print tabloid. You can follow Bat Boy's continuing adventures (along with tales of Obatma, Barack Obama's little-known half-man, half-bat half-brother) on the *Weekly World News* Web site.

Q Can a criminal collect a reward on himself?

A It's highly unlikely, but not impossible. Anyone can offer a reward: the family of a crime victim, a concerned citizens' group, a corporation, and a nonprofit organization such as Crime Stoppers, which pays for anonymous tips. And some local government bodies even offer rewards in certain criminal investigations. But there are no uniform laws or regulations regarding how these rewards are disbursed.

In point of fact, whoever offers the reward gets to decide who can collect the money. Nonetheless, it's difficult to imagine a provision that would allow the perpetrator of the crime to pocket the dough.

The business of rewards can be tricky. A well-publicized, big-money offer sometimes works against an investigation by attracting greedy tipsters who provide useless leads to overworked detectives. Law enforcement agencies generally don't discourage reward offers, but they do try to use them strategically. Often they won't publicize a reward until an investigation nears a dead end, the hope being that it'll renew interest in the crime and jog the memories of legitimate tipsters.

Many police officials concede that offers of a reward rarely lead to a successful investigation. Most useful tips, they say, come from honest citizens with good intentions that go beyond recompense.

And the existence of a reward doesn't necessarily mean the tipsters will know how to collect it. In July 2008, the FBI offered a twenty-five-thousand-dollar reward in its search for Nicholas Sheley, a suspect in a series of killings. Sheley, it seems, walked into a bar in Granite City, Illinois, to get a drink of water. The bar's patrons had seen his face on the TV news. One called the police; another ran outside and flagged down a squad car. Sheley was quickly taken into custody. Four months later, an FBI spokesman said that nobody had stepped forward to collect the twenty-five grand.

Never mind the bad guys. Sometimes even the good guys don't get the money.

Q Whom do we blame for the mullet hairstyle?

A The mullet was rearing its ugly head as long ago as the Trojan War, around 1200 BC. Indeed, the first documented account of the short-hair-around-the-face, long-hair-covering-the-neck-in-back look is in *The Iliad*. Homer relates that the fierce, spear-carrying Abantes warriors wore their tresses long and flowing, but with "their forelocks cropped."

While mullet-like hairstyles have appeared since then (think of Gainsborough's eighteenth-century "Blue Boy" painting), rock stars made it popular in the early 1970s. David Bowie's 1972 Ziggy Stardust character cut his short in front and long in back, and dyed it bright orange to complete the look. Beatles legend Paul McCartney sported a tame mullet when he launched his new band, Wings, in 1971. The style caught on—though it wasn't yet called the mullet.

Men and women, from punky Lou Reed to prissy Florence Henderson, sported variations in the 1970s. In the 1980s, movie stars Brad Pitt and Mel Gibson and TV's Richard Dean Anderson (*MacGyver*) proudly wore mullets. Singers Billy Ray Cyrus and Michael Bolton and tennis ace Andre Agassi were among celebrities who ushered the mullet into the 1990s. By the time David Spade wore one in the 2001 movie *Joe Dirt,* the look had become linked with lounge lizards and ne'er-do-wells. Today, it's affectionately celebrated on several Web sites.

The mullet, which is essentially two haircuts in one, has many names. It's sometimes called the 10/90: 10 percent of the hair in front, 90 percent in back. It's also known as the ape drape, hockey hair, and the Tennessee top hat. "Business up front, party in the back" is both a nickname and a description.

No one is sure who started calling the hairdo a mullet. "Mullet-head" was an insult in Mark Twain's day—it's what he called dimwits in *The Adventures of Huckleberry Finn*—but the term referred to mullet fish. Today, it refers to hair…but it's still kind of an insult.

Q Do Buddhists consider Buddha a god?

A Like Jesus, Buddha was a religious leader who taught disciples spiritual principles and a new way of life. But while Christians view Jesus as the son of God, Buddhists regard Buddha as a human—an incredibly awesome human, but a human nonetheless.

"Buddha" can be a general term meaning "enlightened one," a person who sees existence as it really is. But when people say "Buddha," they usually mean a specific person, Siddhartha Gautama. He was born in Nepal around 563 BC, and his teachings are the origin of Buddhism.

As with any religious figure that lived long ago, historians disagree on the details of Buddha's life. But the general Buddhist belief goes like this: Siddhartha Gautama was the son of a feudal lord and grew up in sheltered luxury. At twenty-nine, after seeing how others suffered, he left his family and devoted himself to understanding the true nature of life. At thirty-five, after years as a homeless ascetic, he sat under a tree and vowed to stay there until he understood the universe. As he meditated, he saw his many past lives and understood the nature of samsara—a cycle of reincarnation that is determined by karma, the positive and negative actions taken in each life. He also saw how to move beyond this cycle of suffering to a higher plain of existence, called nirvana. He dedicated his life to teaching others dharma, the way to achieve enlightenment.

Buddha communicated his core message through four basic truths:

- Life is suffering
- This suffering comes from ignorance of the true nature of life.
- To end the suffering, a person must overcome this ignorance and all attachments to earthly things.

- A person can do this by following the noble eightfold path, generally translated as right views, right intention, right speech, right action, right livelihood, right effort, right mindedness, and right contemplation. (Buddha elaborated on each of the eight paths, but for that, we'd need an entire book.)

Buddhists believe that anyone may achieve nirvana, but the expectation is that only Buddhist monks are in the right position to do so. So Buddhists strive to make progress toward achieving enlightenment in a later life. In some schools of thought, anyone who achieves enlightenment is known as a Buddha; in others, only someone who arrived at nirvana without any guidance is called a Buddha, like Gautama and the Buddhas who came before him.

Buddhists believe that when Buddha died, he achieved parinirvana, the final release from the earthly realm. While this is seen as a transition to a higher state of being, it's very different from the concept of a god, since a Buddha did not create the universe and doesn't control it.

If you want to know what the higher state is all about, you'll have to find out the hard way. Better get cracking on that good karma.

Q Why do guys wear ties?

A There's a reason hangings are often referred to as "necktie parties." A lot of men find neckties to be downright stiff and suffocating. So why wear them? Tradition, baby!

Wearing neck garb is a centuries-old practice that is believed to have begun with Shih Huang Ti, China's first emperor. Shih Huang Ti died in 210 BC, and when he was buried, 7,500 life-size terracotta replicas of his famed fighting force were buried with him. When his massive mausoleum was unearthed near the ancient capital of Xian in 1974, researchers found legions of meticulously carved officers, soldiers, archers, and horsemen guarding the emperor's sarcophagus. Each figure was unique in its armor, hair, and even facial expression. But they were all the same in one respect: Each wore a carefully wrapped silk neck cloth.

Historians say that the Chinese people did not wear neckties at the time, so why the terracotta guards wore them remains a mystery. However, because the cloths were made of silk, one of the world's great luxuries, it's thought that they might have been intended to signify that Shih Huang Ti's soldiers were bestowed with the ultimate badges of honor.

In fact, great fighters have been honored and identified with some version of neckwear throughout history. In AD 113, the Roman emperor Trajan erected a marble column to commemorate a triumphant victory over the Dacians. The column featured 2,500 realistic figures wearing different kinds of neckwear, from knotted kerchiefs to shorter versions of what resemble the modern necktie.

Interestingly, Roman writers like Horace and Seneca had remarked that only effeminate men covered their necks. (They were likely referring to Roman orators who wore neck cloths to keep their throats warm.) However, it's clear that skilled, highly respected soldiers were spared these stereotypical assumptions. It's even said that French king Louis XIV took up the fashion of wearing neck scarves after seeing them on victorious Croatian mercenaries during the Thirty Years' War (1618–1648). After the war, brilliantly colored silk neck scarves became fashionable throughout France, England, Europe, and, later, the United States. And they did have some redeeming utilitarian purposes. They protected the neck and buttons on shirts, and if thick enough, they could possibly stop the thrust of a sword.

Today, of course, neckties are more often worn to add sophistication and color to a man's business suit or formal wear. But they also continue to proclaim status, add austerity, and identify allegiance to a school or group. Modern neckties are available in all kinds of styles, materials, patterns, and colors.

So if an oversize silk paisley is a little too conventional for you, go for a wide-ribbon plantation tie. It's considered to be the first all-American necktie, and it's a look that clearly worked for Mark Twain and Colonel Sanders.

Chapter Two

HEALTH MATTERS

Q **What did they use for birth control in the old days?**

A Tough question. It's not information that got written down—at least not often.

Some hints are found in the ancient writings of doctors and naturalists. They show that fruits and herbs played a big role in controlling fertility. An Egyptian scroll of medical advice that's thirty-five hundred years old tells how to end a pregnancy at any point: Mix the unripe fruit of acacia with honey and other items to be soaked up by an absorbent pad of plant fiber. Insert the pad into the vagina, and an abortion will follow. (Dissolved acacia produces lactic acid, which is a spermicide.)

Other old texts show that herbal birth control was brewed into teas. The leaves of pennyroyal (a type of mint) and parts of many plants that look like weeds to us could be brewed as a "morning-after" cure for unwanted pregnancies. Juniper berries, willow bark, mugwort, aloe, anise, dittany, and certain ferns were all used. Seeds from the plant Queen Anne's lace or from pomegranates were eaten for the same reason, as were figs.

Many of these plant-based solutions were known to people in the Middle Ages and the Renaissance. In Shakespeare's *Hamlet,* Ophelia plays with the herb rue, a weed known to induce abortions. Rue is found throughout the Americas, too, and many native groups used it to end pregnancies.

What about condoms, sponges, and other devices? Illustrations that are thousands of years old show men using condoms, though the earliest condom that's been found dates to 1640. It's made of sheep intestines. Goodyear began mass production of rubber condoms in 1843.

Female condoms, or cervical dams, have also been around for millennia. They've included seedpods, oiled paper, seaweed, lemon or pomegranate halves, beeswax, and even moss. History also records the use of spermicidal potions made from oils, vinegar, rock salt, wine, and herbs.

Superstition and ignorance about the properties of certain ingredients played roles in some of these birth-control methods. Modern research on animals shows that some of these ingredients would have resulted in lower pregnancy rates or increased instances of miscarriage. However, some of these substances also are toxic, which would have made the birth-control benefits moot.

Q Does anyone really slip on a banana peel?

A Think the only people who slip on banana peels are Looney Tunes characters and silent film actors from the 1920s? Well, try telling that to the Florida Supreme Court. In 2001, seven justices from the state's highest tribunal considered two cases in which women took slippery skids upon the peels of bananas.

The first woman, Elvia Soriano, slipped and fell on "a brown, mushy, rotten banana peel" while shopping at the U-Save Supermarket in Palm Beach County in 1992. The second woman, Evelyn Owens, slipped and fell on "a small piece of slightly discolored banana" while perusing the St. Cloud Publix in 1995. Both women sustained injuries—which were likely more serious than a halo of circling birdies—and sued the stores for failing to quickly clean the bananas off their floors.

Now, you may simply assume that these ladies were batty, bonkers, or—okay—bananas. But the truth is, the basic facts of both cases weren't in question. According to court records, it was established that Soriano and Owens had slipped and fallen on the bananas. What had to be proven was exactly how long the bananas had been lying there and just who was responsible for the messes.

Lawyers pointed to a slew of legal disputes surrounding foods that caused shoppers to slip and fall in Florida supermarkets. These unsavory episodes included a 1984 case involving collard green leaves, a 1993 case in which sauerkraut was the culprit, and a 1966 case that centered on yet anther dreaded banana peel.

As it turns out, plantains aren't the only fresh foodstuffs to cause unpredictable pratfalls. The verdict? Watch your step in the produce aisle, particularly when you're shopping for groceries in the Sunshine State.

Q Do weird things happen to an astronaut's body in outer space?

A They sure do. Playing zero-gravity paddleball and cruising around on the surface of the moon may look like good, clean fun, but space travel is no picnic. Astronauts' bodies endure some crazy changes in the celestial firmament, and it takes awhile for them to recover once they're back on solid ground.

So what's the problem? In a word, weightlessness. And the most immediate consequence of the zero-G lifestyle is something that astronauts call space adaptation syndrome. It occurs because the structure of the inner ear that gives you your sense of balance is acclimated to the constant force of gravity; when that force disappears, your inner ear tells you that you're perpetually falling forward. This typically causes nausea, vomiting, dizziness, and disorientation.

There are other, more serious consequences from leaving Earth, and they have to do with gravity's effect on the rest of the body. Here on Earth, we spend our entire lives within the planet's gravitational field. Even when we're not trying to leap over a puddle or pull off a Superman dunk, the force of gravity is constantly compressing our bodies—and, importantly, our bodies are fighting back.

To understand how your body is forever fighting gravity, just think of your circulatory system. The force of gravity tries to pull your blood supply down into your lower extremities; your heart meanwhile works hard against gravity to keep the blood flowing into your upper body, too. If you were to leave Earth's gravitational field, your heart would be working *too* hard at forcing the blood upwards, causing your face to swell and leading to nasal congestion and bulging eyes. But eventually, your body would adjust to its new environment; your heart would pump less intensely and your blood pressure would lower.

And without the force of gravity, your muscles atrophy—they get smaller and weaker. Hardest hit are postural muscles like your hamstrings and back muscles, the ones that fight against gravity to keep you standing tall. But all of your muscles begin to wither, as it requires less effort to make any movement. Even your heart is affected, in part because of your lowered blood pressure. As a perk, your intervertebral discs—essentially shock absorbers for the spine—expand, making you two to three inches taller. But even this height enhancement can be painful.

The biggest problem is the effect of weightlessness on the bones. In order to stay strong enough to meet the demands of daily living, your bones constantly regenerate themselves in accordance with the level of strain that they experience For example, if you lift weights regularly, your bones will grow stronger and more calcium-fortified.

In space, however, the reduced level of stress causes bones to weaken and lose their mass. Studies on astronauts working in Skylab in the 1970s showed a 0.3 percent loss of bone mass during each month of weightlessness.

Due to all of these physical changes, astronauts are in pretty bad shape when they get back home. Their lowered blood pressure can lead to fainting. (To alleviate this problem, they sometimes wear special suits that compress the legs and feet, forcing more blood to the torso and head.) Their sense of balance is out of whack for about a week, making it hard for them to remain steady on their feet. And they're very weak because of the muscle degeneration; it can take months to fully regain lost muscle mass. Bone regeneration can take years, and extended missions—like a three-year Mars trip—would cause permanent bone damage.

It's a lot of wear and tear for the opportunity to hit a golf ball on the moon. Rocketing into space doesn't sound quite as cool anymore, does it?

Q Can leeches and maggots really heal wounds?

A Before the advent of modern medicine, there were some pretty wild treatments for bodily injury, disease, and dysfunction. If you had, say, persistent migraines, you might've tried to get rid of them by having a small hole drilled into your skull. Makes sense, right? And of course, there was the leech— the wormlike parasite that was thought to alleviate a vast number of ailments as it grew fat on a sick person's blood.

The medical community has come a long way since then, but there's still a place for the leech, along with a creature that's arguably even more disgusting, the maggot. In 2004, these two unsavory critters became the first living animals recognized by the U.S. Food and Drug Administration as medical devices.

Thankfully, contemporary doctors don't use leeches as a cure-all blood-drainer like the ancient Greeks and Egyptians and the medieval Europeans did. Today they're used primarily to help patients recover from major reconstructive surgery. As tissue re-forms following a skin graft, blood often drains abnormally, which can lead to swelling. The blood vessels in the ears and other delicate body parts are especially prone to clots that can kill the recovering tissue.

Leeches are a viable solution to these problems because they can drain blood, and their saliva contains more than thirty different proteins that keep blood flowing, numb pain, and reduce swelling. The amazing truth is, they are more effective at these treatments than any alternative that has been tried by modern medical practitioners.

Meanwhile, the maggot—the larval form of the blowfly—is used to treat serious wounds that are infected or gangrenous. Maggots feed on the dead tissue; this effectively cleans the wound and arrests infection, allowing the damaged tissue beneath to heal. The maggots' secret weapon—a secretion of enzymes that turn dead tissue into a digestible mush—is known to help wounds that have resisted all other treatments.

The maggot procedure is an ordeal—and not just for squeamish types. Hundreds of the wriggling insects are applied to the wound and covered with a bandage. After a couple of days, the well-fed maggots are removed and replaced with a hungry group, and the process is repeated until the wound is healed. Sounds gross, huh? Luckily, good old Bactine and Band-Aids get the job done for more minor scrapes and cuts.

Q Does the dentist know I'm lying when I tell him I floss?

A "Have you been flossing?" If your dentist asks this question, we suggest that you find a new tooth-care professional. This one's after some perverse pleasure at your expense.

You're not going to say "no," are you? You'll probably turn red and stammer through some lame excuse about why you haven't been flossing *enough*—You're certain that dentists think no one flosses *enough*. Rather than make you squirm about flossing, all a dentist has to do is take a peek inside your mouth. The answer is there to see. And if you haven't been flossing at all, it's also there to smell.

Flossing is essential to dental hygiene because it clears away plaque and food debris that a toothbrush can't reach. If your teeth haven't been flossed since the last time you were in the dentist's chair, they'll have far more gunk than those of someone who flosses regularly. Flossing also helps to reduce discoloration where your teeth meet, so streaks and staining can give you away as well.

Flossing reduces tooth decay and cavities, combats bad breath, and helps to prevent gum disease. If you don't floss, your gum tissue can become sensitive from the buildup of food and plaque between your gums and teeth. Bleeding gums are also evidence of a lack of flossing.

The lesson here? Floss regularly and you'll be able to answer the dreaded question from your dentist with a brilliant, carefree smile.

Q Can the cold give you a cold?

A No, you won't catch a cold by running around in the frigid air while wearing only underwear (not that we here at F.Y.I. headquarters would ever do such a thing) or traipsing through town with wet hair. Sorry, Mom—and old wives.

While it's true that colds are more prevalent during the nippy months from September to April, the cold temperatures are probably not to blame. These just happen to be the months when viruses are typically spread.

One study did conclude that cold temperatures might indeed give you a cold. Researchers at Cardiff Common Cold Centre in Wales asked 180 volunteers to sit with their feet in bowls of ice-cold water for twenty minutes. Over the next five days, 29 percent of the cold-feet volunteers caught a cold, compared to 9 percent of an empty-bowl control group. It's thought that cold temperatures can constrict the blood vessels of the nose, turning off the warm blood supply to white blood cells (the ones that fight infections).

However, most research continues to show that being physically chilled or wet really has nothing to do with catching a cold. We spend more time indoors during the winter, oftentimes exposed to sniffling coworkers who refuse to take sick days. (Are they still hoping to win a gold star for perfect attendance?) Before you know it, January rolls around and you're drowning in a mound of Puffs Plus and begging someone—anyone—to make you a batch of chicken noodle soup.

Who hasn't been there? That's why it's the "common cold." More than two hundred types of viruses can cause it. There are the rhinovirus (the leading cause of the common cold, made famous in Lysol disinfectant TV commercials), the respiratory syncytial virus, and lots, lots more. These nasty bugs lurk on telephones, cutting boards, computer mice, doorknobs, hand towels, and pretty much everywhere hands are meant to go.

So wipe those areas down with disinfecting sprays or wipes and be vigilant about cleansing your hands with antibacterial soap and water or hand sanitizer gel. Dr. Neil Schachter, author of *The Good Doctor's Guide to Colds and Flu,* says that people who wash their hands seven times a day get 40 percent fewer colds than the average person.

You know what else? It really can't hurt to throw on your ski mask and thermal snowsuit when the temperature dips below freezing. At least it will make your mom feel better.

Q Does the Ouija board really work?

A Hold on, we need to see if our Magic 8 Ball knows the answer: "Ask again later." What? That lazy Magic 8 Ball.

The Ouija board, invented by three or four men in the 1890s, consists of a pointer and a separate board on which is printed the alphabet, numerals zero through nine, and the words "yes," "no," and "goodbye." The inventors claimed that if several people put their hands on the pointer and asked a question, spirits of the dead would guide the pointer to an answer. Depending on where the pointer landed, the answer could be one of the three words printed on the board or a combination of words and numerals.

The inventors obtained a United States patent on the Ouija board, which they cited as proof that it actually worked. Today, toy and game manufacturer Parker Brothers sells the Ouija board as a game (the modern board glows in the dark). Company sales literature describes the Ouija as a "mystifying oracle" but does not say that it's a means of communicating with the dead.

As mysterious as the Ouija board's pointer may seem—it appears to move on its own—its motions are rooted in science. We're referring to the ideomotor effect, the involuntary or unconscious movement of muscles due to the influence of suggestion.

Evidence has demonstrated that a person's brain can pick up signals and instruct muscles to do something without the person being consciously aware of it. The ideomotor effect was introduced in 1852 by the English physiologist William Benjamin Carpenter, although the concept had been discussed since the early eighteen hundreds.

Ouija answers are examples of the ideomotor effect. The game's concept establishes an atmosphere in which participants either expect or want the pointer to move and expect or want the board to answer their questions. The directions instruct a player to place a hand on the pointer and watch as it "answers" a question. The brain picks up on this and reacts accordingly by unconsciously directing the player's arm to move the pointer. The resulting muscle movements can be so minute that the player doesn't even realize they're happening. What would our Magic 8 Ball say about that?

Q Why do people with Tourette's Syndrome curse so much?

A Most of them don't. Fewer than 15 percent of people with Tourette's find themselves compelled by the condition to blurt out profanity, racial epithets, and other offensive language. But why *any* Tourette's sufferer exhibits such behavior is a medical mystery.

Tourette's Syndrome is a condition characterized by one or more pervasive tics—physical actions that are extremely difficult to resist. For a small minority of people with Tourette's, these tics take the form of coprolalia—the uncontrolled use of highly inappropriate language. The majority of Tourette's sufferers experience only non-vocal tics, such as rapid blinking and nose scrunching. Some sufferers utter non-offensive words or repeat words that they just heard.

Scientists don't fully understand what causes Tourette's Syndrome, but they believe that it's related to abnormal levels of particular neurotransmitters, the chemicals in the brain that facilitate signals between neurons. Drugs that reduce levels of dopamine, a neurotransmitter that affects inhibition and motor control, among other things, have lessened the severity of tics for some Tourette's sufferers.

Functional magnetic resonance imaging scans of people with Tourette's show abnormal activity in the basal ganglia, located in the center of the brain. This group of tiny structures is involved in fine motor control, regulating impulsive behavior and managing fear and anger. One theory points specifically to inoperative dopamine receptors in the caudate nucleus. This part of the basal ganglia normally acts as a brake, inhibiting random unconscious impulses.

What exactly does this have to do with uncontrollable swearing? It's really not clear, although evidence suggests that we process offensive words and phrases differently from other language. For most people, curse words are emotionally charged, which might connect them more closely to unconscious impulses. Think of it this way: If a car almost hits you, the chances are fairly good that you'll swear without consciously meaning to. For the Tourette's sufferer, subdued fear, anger, or anxiety might trigger the same reaction.

In any case, if you find yourself on the receiving end of Tourette's-fueled profanity, don't take offense. It's nothing personal.

Q Are old men grumpier than most people?

A From the beginning of time—or roughly sixty years after the beginning of time—they've warmed our hearts with such expressions as, "Get off my lawn!" and "No! No! You're doing it all wrong! Get out of the way, I'll do it myself, you [*grumbling that may not be actual words*]."

They're grumpy old men, and they don't like you. They don't like anything, really. And they like it that way. And whether you like it or not, researchers confirm that grumpy old men are no joke; they're very real victims of their own physiology.

The English Longitudinal Study of Ageing surveyed nearly ten thousand people ages fifty-five and older and asked them to rate themselves in areas such as health, finances, and overall happiness. Across the board, men reported lower levels in quality of life than did women. Why? Are old men uncomfortable in those pants? Does the hair growing from their ears and nostrils irritate them?

The answer may be male menopause. Also known by its clinical name, andropause (or the snicker-inducing hypogonadism), male menopause is caused by testosterone deficiency. Some men experienced diminished testosterone production in their forties; full decline occurs in the early fifties.

The symptoms include flaccidity in a certain body part and an unwillingness to get it on. (See some connection here?) Irritability, depression, and loss of sleep are other signs. Treatments range from simple life changes—such as increased exercise, improved diet, and lowering stress—to chemical enhancements that include elevating testosterone levels through injections or supplements.

Identified by medical researchers as early as the 1940s, male menopause can be difficult for doctors to diagnose. It develops slowly over a long period, so it's tricky to pinpoint. And well . . . *you* try to get a grumpy old man who's sitting on a cold examination table wearing nothing but a paper gown to talk about his feelings.

But male menopause may yet find its way onto center stage. Baby Boomers, accustomed to whining until they get what they want, are beginning to complain about growing old. In the process, the medical community is learning more about male menopause and how to identify and treat it effectively.

Yes, doctors are actually looking forward to the day when seventy-five-year-old men share graphic—and gruesome—details of their sex lives.

Q When you have a fever, why do you feel cold one minute and hot the next?

A Other than getting to miss school and sip Mom's chicken soup, it's no fun to have a fever. Your muscles ache; your appetite vanishes; your energy dissipates; and your body temperature seems to swing between a deep freeze and a nuclear meltdown. You're shuddering under the bed covers one minute and breaking into a profuse sweat the next. But if you think these temperature swings are unpleasant, just imagine how the virus that's attacking your body feels.

A fever is how your body fights contagions that cause infection and illness. Bacteria and viruses have evolved to thrive at normal body temperatures. When they enter your body, the hypothalamus—the part of your brain that regulates body temperature—essentially turns up the heat to drive out the invaders.

Once the hypothalamus calls for a body temperature adjustment, you're thrown into the unpleasantness of the fever cycle. When your body recognizes that it needs to be at a higher temperature, you turn cold and the chills set in; the resulting rapid muscle contractions help warm your body. And because you feel uncomfortably cold, you cuddle under the covers in your pajamas and your body temperature rises even more.

When your body temperature begins to climb above the level prescribed by your hypothalamus, you get hot and sweaty, kick off the covers, and ask for ice water. (You may also feel this way if you take a fever-reducing drug like acetaminophen.) But eventually—unless your body has stamped out the invaders completely—your body will turn the heat back on, bringing back the chills.

As unpleasant as these fluctuations in temperature may be, they create an unstable environment for threatening viruses and bacteria. Unless your fever climbs so high that it threatens to damage your body tissue, there's no need to fight it. Your body is simply doing what it needs to in order to drive out the invader and restore your good health.

Q Is it true that bed bugs bite?

A You better believe they do. In fact, it's pretty much the *only* thing they do.

A brownish-red, flat, and oval-shaped wingless insect, the common bed bug (*Cimex lectularius* if you're a Latin lover) grows to about a quarter-inch in length and feeds exclusively on the blood of animals. This includes you, sleepyhead.

Bed bugs are nocturnal, hiding in cracks and crevices during the day and emerging at night to feed on a host. They use an elongated beak to puncture the skin and can spend three to ten minutes drawing blood. Often, the victim never feels a thing.

If you awake with itchy, reddish welts on your skin, it's possible that you were the main course at a bed-bug feast. But symptoms vary, and some people don't react to the bites at all. Thankfully, under normal circumstances, bites from bed bugs don't spread disease, just a measure of discomfort.

Bed bugs don't prey exclusively on humans—they can also be found around the nests of birds and bats, for example. But they have demonstrated an enduring affinity for people: Literary references to bed bugs date to the days of Aristotle.

The little suckers were on the run in America in the years following World War II, however. The rise of such household cleaning staples as vacuum cleaners and pesticides helped diminish their forces.

But as pesticides with the broad-spectrum killer DDT were replaced by more specialized products aimed specifically at such pests as roaches and ants, bed bugs regained their foothold. And because they travel well in clothing and luggage, they've been slowly reintroduced to North America, notably in hotels (and not just the cheap ones), homes, and hospitals.

"Don't let the bed bugs bite" isn't just a quaint saying. These pesky predators are back in business.

Chapter Three

TRADITIONS

Q Does anyone send a telegram anymore?

A On May 24, 1844, Samuel Morse, inventor of the telegraph and of Morse code, sent this message over an experimental line from Washington, D.C., to Baltimore: "What hath God wrought?" That was the first telegram, and more than 160 years later, young fingers echo the sentiment with every "OMG!" that's punched into a cell phone keyboard. It's an appropriate, albeit unintended, homage—for what was a telegram if not Victorian texting?

Decades before any of today's forms of instantaneous communication existed, the telegram was the quickest way to bother somebody who wasn't within earshot. You'd visit a telegraph office and dictate a message to a telegraph operator. The operator would tap it out on a "key" that transmitted the message over the telegraph wire in Morse code, a series of long and short electric pulses that represent letters and numbers. An operator on the receiving end would then transcribe the code into a printed message. And like magic, your thoughts would reach your intended target within a matter of hours, delivered in person by a uniformed messenger.

This was revolutionary technology at a time when long-distance communication relied on the mail. And it remained popular even after the advent of the telephone. Western Union, the company most identified with the telegram, sent more than two hundred million of them in 1929. People used them to convey news of births, deaths, and marriages; some pleaded for money, others offered congratulations. The printed messages often were saved for years as markers of life's big events.

But the world has changed considerably since then. In this day of email, the BlackBerry, video conferencing, and other technologies that keep us wired in, does anybody still send a telegram? Bowing to dwindling demand, Western Union stopped telegram service in January 2006. Western Union delivered only about twenty thousand telegrams in its final year.

But the telegram isn't dead. There are still businesses that will deliver one for you, and there are a few remote places in the world where you can stumble across a telegraph office, such as small Balkan villages in Eastern Europe, where electricity and phones are relatively scarce. And you can be sure that people are still asking for money.

Q Why do superheroes wear capes and tights?

A Sure, it's embarrassing to prance around in your pajamas— and worse, with your underpants on the outside—a silly cape flapping behind you. But if it compels criminals to laugh themselves to death, that's good, right?

Cartoonists borrowed the standard superhero outfit—colored tights, trunks, boots, and a cape—from circus strongmen and

professional wrestlers of the early twentieth century. The outfits certainly made sense at the time. Performers needed tight clothing for maximum flexibility and to give the audience a good look at their muscles. However, lycra and elastic had not been invented; with so much squatting and stretching, performers ran the risk of splitting their tights and exposing their...uh... little strongmen. So the thinking performer wore trunks over the tights to keep things family-friendly. And this was show business, so flashy colors were essential.

This ensemble also worked in early comic books. An illustrator had to show off the hero's muscles, but the character couldn't be running around shirtless—it wasn't proper. A skintight outfit delivered the goods without being offensive. And with some unique colors and a chest emblem, the hero was instantly recognizable.

For flying heroes such as Superman, a cape flapping in the wind provides a perfect way to illustrate both speed and direction.

And, of course, folks wore capes back in the day on the planet Krypton.

Q Why do suit jackets have buttons on the sleeves?

A Today, they're purely decorative—only the fanciest custom-tailored suits have buttons on the sleeves that you can fasten and unfasten. And if you believe one popular legend, they were never intended to button anything in the first place.

The popular story goes that the eighteenth-century British naval commander Lord Horatio Nelson (or, in another version of the tale, eighteenth-century Prussian leader Frederick the Great) got tired of the men and boys under his command soiling their uniforms by wiping their noses on the sleeves. To encourage them to use their handkerchiefs instead, he had buttons sewn onto the tops of uniform sleeves (it's not much fun to scrape your nose with big brass buttons). The look caught on, and sleeve buttons jumped from military jackets to regular menswear, eventually migrating from the top of the sleeve to the side.

It's doubtful that this is the true origin of sleeve buttons. Artwork that predates Nelson and Frederick shows buttons on the sleeves of men's garments, and there are some surviving examples of older buttoned-up sleeves. The most famous is the pourpoint (originally, a padded jacket worn under armor) of the nobleman Charles de Blois, which dates back to the 1360s. "Pourpoint" means "for points" and refers to metal tips on laces that hang from the garment, which held up the hose worn under the armor.

De Blois's pourpoint was designed to be tight around the arms and waist, presumably because it had to fit under armor and protect the body with padding. In the days before Spandex, there was no way to make tight clothing that you could just slip on—the cloth wasn't stretchy enough. Instead, you had to fasten yourself into any tight garment. In the case of De Blois's pourpoint, the solution was to sew buttons down the front and along the back of the sleeve, all the way up past the elbow (Charles's pourpoint had twenty buttons). The wearer stuck his arms through the tops of the sleeves, and his assistants helped him button up the lower part of the sleeves to cinch him in.

It became fashionable to wear a pourpoint separate from a suit of armor. Combined with matching chausses à plain frond (the two legs of hose sewn together, with a fabric flap covering the crotch), the outfit was the equivalent of a man's suit today. Most likely, historical fashionistas appreciated the look of the pourpoint's sleeve buttons and kept them around after skintight sleeves went out of style.

Thank goodness they cut the number of buttons from twenty to three or four. Otherwise, businessmen would be getting snagged on things all day long.

Q Why are in-laws the butt of so many jokes?

A Feel beleaguered after a visit with the in-laws? Your situation is hardly unique. The phenomenon spans cultures, generations, and even millennia. Nearly two thousand years ago, the Roman poet Juvenal quipped, "Give up all hope of peace so long as your mother-in-law is alive."

Even then, the mother-in-law joke was told from the son-in-law's perspective. But the real victims of internecine in-law relations are daughters-in-law. Dr. Terri Apter, stressed-out daughter-in-law and Cambridge University psychologist, conducted a twenty-year study of the familial interactions of forty-nine couples and a large number of other people. More than 60 percent of the women reported strained relationships with their female in-laws. On the other hand, only about 15 percent of mother-in-law/son-in-law relationships generated dissatisfaction.

About two-thirds of the daughters-in-law Apter studied claimed that their mothers-in-law were jealous of them. Not surprisingly, roughly the same proportion of mothers-in-law complained of being excluded by their sons' wives. Why are in-law divisions especially prevalent among women?

Apter points to a couple of sources of tension: First, a mother-son relationship is a special bond, and the mother often feels her role being usurped when a new woman enters the picture. Then there's the daughter-in-law's struggle to establish competence in areas that often define women within families—childcare, cooking, maintenance of the home—and trying to do so in the shadow of her more experienced mother-in-law.

Men, Apter says, are often oblivious to the power struggle raging around them. Even if they recognize it, they're adept at feigning ignorance or laughing it off rather addressing the problem. Maybe it's no coincidence that the name of that smart-aleck Roman poet was Juvenal rather than, say, Mature.

Q Why is the rainbow a symbol of gay and lesbian pride?

A In legend and lore, the rainbow represents many things, from goddesses to good luck. In 1978, it became a symbol of gay and lesbian pride. That was the year San Francisco artist Gilbert Baker designed a brilliant eight-color Rainbow Flag for the San Francisco Gay and Lesbian Freedom Day Parade.

According to Baker, each color on the striped flag represented an aspect of the gay and lesbian community: hot pink for sexuality, red for life, orange for healing, yellow for sun, green for nature, turquoise for art, indigo for harmony, and violet for spirit. For the first parade, the artist and thirty volunteers hand-dyed and hand-stitched two huge Rainbow Flag prototypes, each thirty feet by sixty feet. For the following year's event, Baker went to San Francisco's Paramount Flag Company to have the flag mass produced. Hot pink was dropped because it could not be commercially reproduced, and indigo was eliminated to sustain an even number of stripes.

These changes made the Rainbow Flag no less poignant, however. The six-color version spread from San Francisco to other cities and countries, and today it's the most recognizable emblem of the LGBT (lesbian, gay, bisexual, and transgender) community. It hangs in LGBT-friendly neighborhoods, villages, and business districts; it flies freely at gay rallies, demonstrations, and pride events.

In 1994, thousands of volunteers carried a Rainbow Flag measuring thirty-feet-wide by one-mile-long down New York's First Avenue to commemorate the 1969 Stonewall Riots, a confrontation with police that marked the beginning of the gay-rights movement. For the Rainbow Flag's twenty-fifth anniversary in 2003, Baker crafted a record-breaking mile-and-a-quarter-long banner using the original eight colors. Unfurled in Florida at PrideFest Key West, the colors of this rainbow stretched from the Atlantic Ocean to the Gulf of Mexico.

Q Why do professors wear blazers with elbow patches?

A Just as soldiers are clad in fatigues and New York Yankees players wear pinstripes, the brave souls who enter the cutthroat arena of academia don the vestments of their own venerable field. For college professors all over the world, this means, of course, a blazer with elbow patches. As ubiquitous among them as the petty need to undermine the achievements of their colleagues, the jacket with patched elbows has become the standard (if unofficial) uniform for academics. But where did this fashion statement come from in the first place? God knows, people can't wear these things because they look cool.

According to noted fashion writer Bruce Boyer, the impetus to reinforce the elbow of a tweed jacket with a leather patch was born purely of necessity. As it happens, college teachers in the United Kingdom would routinely receive ye olde shaft when it came to their salaries; some educators earned little more than room and board. Professors struggling to make ends meet would naturally try to wring an extra season or two out of their already disheveled attire by patching up any wear and tear. The elbows were the first area of the jacket to wear thin—no doubt from long hours spent leaning over a lectern while pontificating on the world's weighty issues—but leather patches were also often applied to the cuffs, lapels, and button holes.

This professorial parsimony seems sensible enough—we can all understand the impulse to save a few bucks here and there. But it still doesn't explain why brand new jackets are sold with the leather elbow patches already in place. Perhaps this is just a genteel instance of our apparent appetite for pre-distressed clothing. One can enter any mall in America and purchase jeans that have been designed to look well worn even when new—not just "broken in," but completely mangled with carefully placed rips and tears. We're really all just cattle waiting for the next fashion trend to sweep through the high-density feedlot.

Q Why is the day after Thanksgiving called Black Friday?

A For most sane, rational humans, the day after Thanksgiving is best spent in the comfort and quiet of home. They know that venturing out can quickly turn into a nightmare. The stores open at 4:00 AM, but even this isn't early enough for the mindless consumers who camp out overnight in frigid weather to get a first crack at discounts on the gifts du jour. Escalators are jammed, grown adults shove each other out of the way to get to the toy section, and parking lots resemble a bumper car rink at the county fair.

This orgy of consumerism is popularly termed Black Friday, and anybody unfortunate enough to have to travel—or God forbid, run errands—on the day after Thanksgiving can appreciate the appropriateness of such a sobriquet. Nothing can more aptly describe the mood of somebody caught in post-Thanksgiving traffic.

Where the term "Black Friday" originated is the subject of a couple of theories. The one most commonly given in filler newspaper articles is that this is the busiest shopping day of the year and pushes retail stores into profitability—or, in accounting terms, into the black. It's a pithy explanation, but there's no real evidence to support it. Indeed, according to the International Council of Shopping Centers, the day after Thanksgiving isn't the busiest shopping day of the year; that honor is usually reserved for one of the days right before Christmas.

The true origin of Black Friday is rooted in a deeper tradition than post-holiday sales. The concept of terming days of the week as "black" dates back to at least the Fisk-Gould scandal of 1869, when on September 24—known as Black Friday—plunging gold prices left many investors ruined. The same type of color coding was used again during the 1929 stock market crash, when not one, not two, but three days were black—Black Thursday, Black Monday, and Black Tuesday—and history books are filled with photos of Wall Street investors cramming the streets during this economic disaster. It's possible that this imagery led to the current usage of Black Friday.

According to dialect historians, the day after Thanksgiving was called Black Friday in the mid-1960s by Philadelphia policemen who dreaded the vast, slavering crowds that they were sure to encounter. Black Friday took on an even darker connotation on the day after Thanksgiving in 2008. Shoppers at a Wal-Mart in Valley Stream, New York, were so impatient to get to the bargains that they broke down the doors and shoved their way into the store, trampling an employee to death.

Q Why does the woman take the man's last name when they marry?

A It once was a given that a woman would take her husband's last name—patriarchal traditions in English-speaking countries gave her little choice.

A typical family unit placed the man as the head of the household, with both responsibility for and authority over his wife and children. When a girl was born, she became a member of her father's line and was given his last name. Upon marrying, her primary roles became those of wife and the mother of her husband's children. She also became her husband's responsibility and often was considered his property. It stood to reason, then, that she would assume his last name.

Most people in England didn't even have last names until the eleventh century; they typically were known by first names and by their professions or titles. Nobility and royalty began to adopt last names to determine property and title succession around the time of the Domesday Book, a survey of English citizens that was completed in 1086. The practice of passing last names through the father's family trickled down to the lower classes and became the standard in lands colonized and ruled by England.

As the roles of women evolved, so did the practice of automatically taking the man's last name upon marriage. In the 1850s,

American suffragist Lucy Stone first raised the issue of married women retaining their last names, also known as maiden names. A few women followed her suggestion, but most hewed to tradition. As increasing numbers of women forged professional careers and identities away from the home in the twentieth century, more kept their maiden names after marriage. By the 1980s, about 20 percent of married women were retaining their unmarried last names.

But the trend is swinging back the other way. Today, about 10 percent of women keep their maiden names after marriage. Some women hyphenate it with their husband's last name; some couples choose a completely different last name; and in rare instances, a husband will take the last name of his wife. How's that for progress?

Q Why do phone numbers on TV shows and in movies start with 555?

A In 1988, the British pop band Squeeze released the single "853-5937." The phone number in the title had once belonged to the band's lead singer, Glenn Tilbrook, and the song was based on a jingle that he had used on his answering machine.

The single climbed the charts and became one of Squeeze's few U.S. hits. Good news for the band; bad news for anyone else who happened to have that phone number. Around the country, annoyed citizens reported receiving up to fifty calls a day from fans hoping to speak to members of Squeeze. Some of the callers became combative when told that no one from the band was at that number—never mind that the members of Squeeze lived on an entirely different continent.

And this, in a nutshell, is why phone numbers referenced in TV shows and movies usually start with 555: As the Squeeze example illustrates, a surprising number of people are idiots. The moment that a phone number is mentioned—even in passing—on any television show or movie, you can rest assured that some jackass is frantically punching the numbers into his phone. (The same thing happened in 1980 when the band Tommy Tutone hit number four on the charts with a song that had the number 867–5309 in its chorus.)

So what makes 555 numbers immune to this problem? For years, numbers beginning with 555 had been reserved by the phone company for special use—most notably, 555–1212 for directory assistance. Few other 555 numbers had ever been assigned, so scriptwriters felt comfortable using made-up 555 numbers to idiot-proof their productions.

In 1994, the agency that assigns phone numbers—the North American Numbering Plan Administration—decided to start offering 555 numbers to the general public. The idea was to turn the 555 exchange into something like the 800 prefix—easily accessible from any area code and (theoretically) attractive to businesses that wanted easy-to-remember phone numbers. Mindful of the ever-present danger of idiots, the administrators reserved a range of numbers—555–0100 to 555–0199—for use in works of fiction.

For what it's worth, Squeeze hated "853–5937" about as much as the unwitting victims of the song did. "I hold myself solely responsible for this utter waste of time," Tilbrook would declare years later in the book *Squeeze: Song by Song*. That said, he did relish the annoyance that his song created: "We made the front page of *USA Today* because so many irate people were getting calls. That was the only good thing about the song."

Q Why don't Scotsmen wear underwear beneath their kilts?

A Except for on a few formal occasions, no one tells these guys that they need underwear. It's their choice, and to the consternation and/or amusement of the rest of the Western world, many Scotsmen choose not to wear undershorts with their kilts.

This harks back to the rough-and-tumble origins of the kilt—to the late sixteen hundreds or earlier, in the dark age before mankind had invented briefs, boxers, boxer-briefs, or Marky Mark, when the kilt was basically a huge bolt of wool that men wrapped around themselves in numerous ways, including as a shawl or a blanket.

Several Scottish military regiments stipulate that no underwear be worn unless there is a chance that things could get exhibitionist—like if you're marching in a pipe band (where knees are raised) or participating in the Highland games (where piping, drumming, dancing, and athletic contests take place). Not wearing underwear is called "military practice" or "going regimental," an idiom that is similar to the American expression "going commando," which refers to soldiers skipping the Skivvies in order to save rucksack space, stay cooler, avoid having to wash under-wear, and prevent skin rashes and other nether issues.

Kilt-wearers—either civilians or soldiers—who do wear undies can buy them from makers of special underwear. These garments match the kilt patterns or are complementary in color. Another option is to wear boxers, briefs, or even Lycra shorts.

Again, the men in kilts usually make these vital decisions about their vitals. This unusual freedom only adds to the mystique of the Scottish soldier, who has been known throughout history as rug-ged to the point of uncouth—so secure in his manhood, in other words, that he doesn't care what goes on down there.

Q Why do soldiers salute?

A The military depends on deeply ingrained rituals in order to accomplish just about everything it does. The horrors of combat can become even worse if military personnel fail to follow orders to the tee or waver in their service and mission. Even in less-intense situations, such as the close quarters of everyday military life, maintaining a strictly enforced sense of decorum is critical.

So members of the armed forces of the United States salute as a way of regularly reinforcing their respect for the chain of com-mand, for the country, and for each other. This simple gesture is one of many matters of formal courtesy woven into the fabric of the military.

Militaries of other countries follow similar practices, though the details may vary. They're all honoring a custom that goes back so far that no one is certain how it got started. Nevertheless, two explanations are likely:

Many historians believe that civilians in ancient Rome raised their right hands when approaching military officers or other public officials. This was originally a way of showing that the civilian wasn't preparing to stab the official with a dagger (assassinations were something of a problem in ancient Rome).

Other historians believe that medieval knights in full armor raised their visors when approaching each other to signal that they meant no harm. This became a sign of respect, and it evolved into touching the brim of the hat or removing the hat, and, finally, into a version of the modern salute.

Today, each branch of the United States military has specific guidelines for when saluting is appropriate. As a general rule, members of the armed forces salute all officers in any branch of the U.S. military or any allied military whenever they are in uniform and outdoors. The lower-ranking person is supposed to salute first, and then the higher-ranking officer returns the gesture.

In addition, members of the military are expected to salute the president, who is also commander in chief of the armed forces, and any recipient of the Medal of Honor. Saluting is mandatory when raising or lowering the flag; during the national anthem and when other ceremonial music is played; when rendering reports; and during particular ceremonies, such as funerals and changes of command.

Because guidelines for each branch get a little complicated, saluting when it's not absolutely required is generally acceptable. Failing to salute when it's expected, on the other hand, is considered deeply disrespectful.

Q Why are most pencils yellow?

A Because yellow pencils work better. Ask anyone. Studies in the United States show that people generally prefer the performance of a yellow-painted pencil over a pencil of a different hue—even if they're made from identical lead and wood. How did we get so brainwashed?

In the late nineteenth century, the L & C Hardtmuth Company of Budweis, Bohemia (at the time, a territory of the Austro-Hungarian Empire and today a part of the Czech Republic), decided to manufacture a pencil that would be superior to all others, in performance as well as in price.

Reportedly, the designers of the pencil wanted to show their patriotism by incorporating the colors of the Austro-Hungarian flag, gold and black, into their new product. The pencil's graphite center was black, so they painted the top-of-the-line writing instrument yellow to complete the effect.

Now it was time to choose a name for this Rolls-Royce of pencils. Hardtmuth was inspired by a stunning diamond that had recently been presented to England's Queen Victoria—the Koh-I-Noor diamond. He reasoned that both the diamond and the pencil were "gems" that were made from carbon. Koh-I-Noor pencils were introduced in 1890 and became a top-selling writing instrument, and they remain in widespread use.

The Koh-I-Noor certainly made yellow the color of choice for pencils, but it didn't blaze that trail. Yellow pencils date back to at least 1854. An article published in an art magazine that year reported that while most pencils were varnished, some were painted yellow, blue, or black.

So what was so special about the Koh-I-Noor? Each one received fourteen coats of yellow lacquer, and its name was applied in gold leaf. Specially bred cats guarded the Siberian graphite leads against the nibbles of mice until the materials could be placed inside cedar tubes. In short, this was a classy pencil.

Today, Koh-I-Noor Hardtmuth is still a stellar name in writing and art supplies—and yellow is still synonymous with pencils.

Chapter Four

LOVE AND LUST

Q Can men and women truly be "just friends"?

A Sure, but a lot has to stand in the way of "not just friends" before "just friends" can happen. It boils down to what Alan S. Miller and Satoshi Kanazawa write in *Why Beautiful People Have More Daughters*: "The underlying motive of all human behavior is reproductive; reproductive success is the purpose of all biological existence, including humans. Humans do much of what they do, directly or indirectly...to achieve reproductive success." In other words, you and your coworker might be talking about an Excel spreadsheet, but your genes are talking about having babies.

This can be expressed in a number of ways. Maybe you flirt. Maybe you don't flirt, but you're really friendly. Maybe you're not so much friendly as professional, but secretly you're both thinking, "Would I?" and probably answering, "Sure." Your pastor can tell you this is bad, society can tell you this is bad, and no doubt your spouse would gripe if he or she knew about it. But your genes know no better, and they can't help it. All they know is what has worked for hundreds of thousands of years—and, hey, if it ain't broke why fix it?

Does this answer the question? In a way. Let's say that two people would like to be more than just friends, but circumstances prevent it. Depending on how compelling these circumstances are—say, they're committed to other people or they aren't allowed to have workplace romances—they can subdue the impulse to be more than just friends.

But every step of the way, they're fighting an uphill battle against their genes. And the genes often have an uncanny way of winning out.

Q Who throws the bouquet at a gay wedding?

A You know the drill: It's the end of the reception, and before the bride gets whisked away in a car decked out with streamers and soda cans, she's supposed to toss her wedding bouquet. A crowd of still-too-young flower girls, single bridesmaids (who are always the bridesmaids), and cat-ladies-in-waiting gather on the dance floor. They pose and preen and elbow each other while jockeying for position—all in hopes of catching an airborne spray of carnations and dendrobium orchids.

But just who gets the honor of slinging that nosegay when the couple is gay? Well, let's just say right off the bat that a gay couple would have much better taste than to select a bouquet of carnations and orchids. The two lovebirds might go with more dramatic flowers, such as calla lilies, gladioluses, or alstroemerias. Furthermore, they would arrange the bouquet by themselves. Fabulous!

But back to the original query. In a same-sex marriage, there may be two grooms, two brides, or even a "bride" and a "groom," meaning that the couple may choose to dress according to society's heterosexual wedding customs (one in a suit, one in a dress). In other words, there may be no bouquets, one bouquet, or even two—it all depends on what the couple chooses to do. When lesbian singer-songwriter Melissa Etheridge married Tammy Lynn Michaels in 2003, they both carried bridal bouquets of hydrangeas and roses.

So in a wedding with two brides, do they both get to throw their bouquets? Why not? It would give *two* single women in the crowd the good fortune of being married next. Maybe even to each other.

Q Are women's breasts getting bigger?

A In the 1930s, the Warner Brothers Corset Company came up with an ingenious idea for promoting its new line of brassieres. Women had complained for years and years about how difficult it was to find a bra that fit right. Think about it: Small women might have large breasts, and large women might have small breasts; some have breasts shaped like apples, while others have breasts shaped like pears or lemons or melons. Breasts come in all shapes and sizes, but in the days of yore, bras didn't. Warner Brothers addressed this nagging problem by creating the "cup size," which ranged from A for the flat-chested to D for the well-endowed.

Sex has never been the same. Cup size isn't simply a marking on a garment tag—no, it's shorthand for colorful and provocative adjectives such as "lubricious" and "bodacious." If *People* reports that a celebrity is a double-D, we know that the magazine isn't referring to her shoe size.

But double-D isn't as big as it gets—not by a long shot. Today's women are wearing bras with E, F, and even G cups. Of course, with the popularity of plastic surgery, it's easy to assume that these women have breast implants. This, however, isn't always the case—many of these super-endowed ladies came by their assets naturally. It appears that women's breasts are indeed getting bigger.

This trend first came to the media's attention in 2007, when the staid British clothing store Marks & Spencer announced it would start stocking bras with J cups in response to burgeoning demand.

More than one-fourth of their lingerie customers wore a D cup or above, and many of those sought EE, FF, or HH.

How do women in other countries measure out? A 2001 market survey of seven European countries revealed that Dutch women ages thirty to thirty-nine had made the biggest gains—more than 30 percent wore D cups or larger. In the United States, the average bra size rose from 34B to 36C between 1996 and 2007.

Why so many bulging breasts? Well, people are getting bigger in general. According to the U.S. Centers for Disease Control and Prevention, the average American woman in 2002 was five-foot-four and weighed 164.3 pounds, an increase of one inch and almost twenty-five pounds over the average American woman in 1960.

People in developed nations grow up eating high-calorie foods, and that translates into increased body fat. Because breasts consist largely of fatty tissue, any increase in body fat is most likely to show up there. Birth control pills and patches containing estrogen can also stimulate breast growth. Exercise, especially weight-lifting, may influence breast size, too—not because it makes breasts bigger, but because it builds the pectoral muscles responsible for supporting them.

Before you start gearing up for the premiere of *The Invasion of the Massive Chests,* be aware that breasts, like everything else, go in and out of fashion. While one generation of women seeks bras that show off breasts to their fullest, another desires garments that make a chest look smaller. The ideal breast size, like beauty, is in the eye of the beholder. And remember, guys—either way, it's not polite to stare.

Q Do women really want to marry a guy who's just like dear old Dad?

A Depends what you mean by "just like." Ask a woman if she wants a man as dependable, kind, and quietly confident as dear old Dad, and the chances are good that she'll say yes. Ask if she wants a man who *looks* like dear old Dad, and she'll probably say, "Huh?" or "Eww!"

Nonetheless, dear old Dad may be a little hotter than some women are willing to admit. According to a couple of studies by European researchers, many women fall for men who look like their fathers, whether they intend to or not. Scientists have dubbed it "sexual imprinting."

Researchers at Hungary's University of Pécs measured proportions of the facial features of members of fifty-two families. Based on this data, they found that the faces of young men and their

fathers-in-law had some strong resemblances, most notably around the nose and eyes. Comparable results came out of a similar study conducted jointly by Durham University in England and the University of Wroclaw in Poland.

For the record, the Oedipal implications of the findings extend to men as well: Most guys go gaga for girls who resemble Mom. The studies found that resemblances between young women and their mothers-in-law occurred in the lips and jaw. (Insert mother-in-law-mouth joke here.)

Scientists offered no substantive explanations for why we choose mates who look like our parents. However, it seems that the likelihood of a woman choosing a man who looks like her father depends on her relationship with him—if the relationship tends to be negative, the woman might stray to other facial types.

Sure, laugh at Pops when he emerges from the bathroom scratching his posterior and belching like a hippo. But to many women, dear old Dad's still got it goin' on—whether they admit it or not.

Q Do Dutch couples always split the bill?

A Ah, to be a male in Amsterdam. Legalized marijuana? Check. Legalized prostitution? Check. Wooden shoes? Check again. And as if this weren't enough, conventional wisdom holds that dating is considerably cheaper in Holland—at least if the phrases "going Dutch" and "Dutch treat" have any validity.

Although some Americans today might think of the Netherlands (the official name for Holland) as a country of tulips and debauchery, this wasn't always the case. For a brief period in the seventeenth century, Holland was one of the world's most powerful empires, largely due to its early exploitation of spice-producing lands in Asia and the Pacific. Along with its financial and military might, Holland saw a cultural flowering during this period, with painters like Rembrandt and Vermeer churning out masterpieces and scientists like Christiaan Huygens laying the foundation for the theory of light. (We're told this was important.)

Of course, Holland wasn't the only imperial nation in the seventeenth century. Most of the other European countries were also getting busy plundering and looting the rest of the world. England, one of the biggest offenders, didn't like the fact that Holland was horning in on its territory. The British expressed their displeasure by waging not one, not two, but three wars against the Netherlands during the seventeenth century. Unfortunately for the British, they were forced to an unsatisfying draw in the first and were soundly whipped in the next two.

Unable to defeat the Dutch in battle, they did the next best thing: They made fun of them. During the seventeenth century, a series of phrases deriding the Dutch worked their way into the English language, such as "Dutch concert" (pandemonium), "Dutch courage" (alcohol), "Dutch comfort" (no comfort at all), and "Dutch feast" (when the host of a dinner gets hammered before the guests even arrive). Most of these phrases have gone the way of the Dutch flotilla, but one has made its way through the centuries to our modern lexicon: "going Dutch" or "Dutch treat," meaning that everyone pays his or her own way.

"Dutch treat" regained popularity in the United States in the late nineteenth century, when xenophobic Americans spewed invectives at German immigrants whom they mistakenly referred to as Dutch (a mispronunciation of the German word *deutsch,* which translates to "German"). Back then, it was considered cheap and rude to make somebody pay his or her own share for an outing that you suggested. Today, however, "going Dutch" is standard in most situations, and it's becoming increasingly so in dating etiquette.

Besides, there isn't any real reason to make fun of the Dutch anymore. By the eighteenth century, Holland's military power had waned and the country slowly receded from the world stage. Holland remains notable, however, for its progressive social policies, such as decriminalized marijuana, same-sex marriages, and socialized health care. Though we're not sure we want to know what "Dutch medicine" entails.

Q Do women weaken legs?

A This question is at once fallacious and fascinating. And by the way, it has to do with sex—and the ages-old nugget that having sex with a woman weakens a man's legs for the next day's athletic competition.

Why is it fallacious? Well, who needs to ask an expert? If the sex is particularly vigorous—more vigorous than an athlete's training regimen—of course it will leave him a little tired. Marathon runners don't do heavy workouts the day before a race; basketball players prefer not to play games two days in a row. You get the idea: Exertion is exertion, and sex can be pretty tiring on a body, legs included. So sure, sex could weaken a man's legs—or a woman's, for that matter (just use your imagination).

That doesn't mean there's a shortage of speculation about the topic, learned and lay, if you'll pardon the expression. Luminaries from the world of sports, including German soccer coach Berti Vogts and British sprinter Linford Christie, have warned against night-before sex. Vogts went so far as to ban sex for his team before the 1994 World Cup. And in the movie *Rocky,* the boxer's trainer, Mickey, barks, "Women weaken legs."

Vogts and Christie were focused on exertion, as was Mickey. But the fictional trainer also was tapping into the notion that there's something mysterious and debilitating about women. This should offend anyone with a clear head. Heck, Casey Stengel, the famous baseball manager, saw through it. He even seemed to believe that sex was uplifting. "Being with a woman all night never hurt no professional baseball player," Casey said. "It's staying up all night looking for a woman that does him in." Moreover, some experts say that sex increases aggressiveness. Others believe that sex decreases aggressiveness the next day, which actually could be good for an athlete prone to over-eagerness.

Regardless, women seem to get the last laugh here. At least one expert has said that women athletes perform better the day after experiencing an orgasm—in fact, the more orgasms the better. For whatever reason, this doctor, the Israeli Alexander Olshanietzky, said that sex works best for high-jumpers and runners. So much for weakened legs—at least for women.

Q Why are there only two sexes?

A Aren't dating and marriage complicated enough as it is? Imagine having to contend with dozens of genders. We'd never stop yelling at each other. But if you put relationship difficulties aside, it seems like it would make better sense to have a plethora of sexes—or maybe even just one.

Biologically speaking, the top priority in life is to reproduce. In a species with only two sexes, you can mate with only 50 percent of the population, assuming the sexes are distributed equally. If you added a third sex, you could mate with two-thirds of the population. If there were ninety-nine different sexes, you could mate with 99 percent of population. And in a species with only one sex, you could mate with 100 percent of the population. From this point of view, two is actually the worst possible number of sexes for finding a mate. Why, then, are almost all animal species comprised of two sexes?

According to the leading theories, human beings and other animals are divided into two sexes because of specialized biological machines called "mitochondria." These microscopic power plants exist inside all of your cells, converting the chemical energy stored in the food that you eat into a form of energy that your body can use. Without mitochondria, life as we know it could not exist.

Mitochondria share many of their features with primitive bacteria—in fact, scientists now suggest that our mitochondria actually evolved *from* bacteria, millions and millions of years ago. The prevailing theory is that, in the far-off mists of time, a single-celled organism engulfed a bacterium, probably in an attempt to eat it.

But instead, the two worked out a symbiotic relationship—the organism gave food to the bacterium, which, in turn, produced a vast amount of energy that the organism could use to sustain a higher level of development.

Even though our mitochondria seem to have once been an independent form of life, they are now firmly integrated as components of our cells. But there's still a genetic holdover from their bacterial origin. Normally when we think of DNA, we picture the genetic information inscribed on the chromosomes inside the nuclei of our cells—the genetic material that determines our hair and skin and eye colors, shapes our personalities, and controls the creation of almost every component of our cells. Every component, that is, except those mysterious mitochondria. That's because each mitochondrion has its *own* internal DNA (called mitochondrial DNA or mtDNA), stored on a simple loop. It's more like the primitive DNA of bacteria than the complex chromosomes in the nucleus of a cell.

Another major difference between your mitochondrial DNA and your normal DNA is that you inherit your mtDNA entirely from your mother (and from her mother, and from her mother's mother, and so on). This has led scientists to theorize that there's a serious evolutionary advantage—although they don't agree on what exactly it is—if only one parent's mtDNA is passed on to the couple's offspring. According to this theory, the biological differences between the two sexes first emerged as a way to ensure that only one parent in a couple could give mtDNA to the next generation.

In early organisms, the differences between the two sexes—let's call them passers and non-passers—were slight. But over millions and millions of years of evolution, the organisms became incredibly more complex and each of the two sexes grew increasingly distinct. Eventually, the passers became female and the non-passers were male.

There are a few species with multiple versions of males—not quite a third sex, but close. For example, certain species of harvester ant have one type of male with sperm that produces worker ants and another type that is designed to make queen ants. At any rate, the basic two-sex system works fine for most species.

Q Why do we say "head over heels in love"?

A You can coo this phrase to your lover when the mood strikes, but let's hope that neither of you thinks about it literally. After all, the sentiment is pretty mundane, even flatly obvious—we spend almost every waking moment with our heads over our heels. So what's so special about you, Romeo?

You might as well say, "I'm so crazy about you that I often find myself seated comfortably upright" or "You're on my mind so much lately that I routinely get eight hours of sleep, three square meals a day, and a reasonable amount of exercise." Regardless of what common sense tells you the phrase should describe, "head over heels" is commonly understood to mean something quite the opposite. Much like "topsy turvy" or "upside down," it's supposed to convey an air of craziness or an unsettled equilibrium.

The original version of the phrase, dating to the fourteenth century, is much more accurate: "heels over head." It was used to describe the precarious moment that you experience while turning a somersault or a cartwheel, when your heels are quite literally suspended over your head. How this got corrupted is anybody's guess, but by the late seventeen hundreds, the more prosaic "head over heels" began to appear in literature. The earliest identified use of the phrase to describe being in love came in 1834, in Davy Crockett's *Narrative of the Life of Davy Crockett.*

Does it make much sense? No. But neither does love—it's the most confusing and illogical of human emotions. So in that respect, the words are perfect just the way they are.

Q Is kissing overrated?

A Ready for a big, sloppy smack to your ego? If you don't like kissing, you're probably doing it wrong. That's right—it takes two to tongue-o, but only one to make a lip-lock flop.

Think back to that first smooch with Sally or Davy in the fifth grade. Remember the clanking teeth, the way-too-invasive tongue, the vacuum-tight seal? That kiss was all sorts of wrong. And all sorts of things can lead to the letdown: lack of know-how, overzealousness, under-zealousness, bologna breath.

Want to experience a kiss that sends shivers down the spine and fireworks into the sky? Consult a professional. Not that kind of professional—more like world-renowned "kissing scholar" William Cane, author of the international bestseller *The Art of Kissing.* Cane (a.k.a. "The Kissing Doctor") says that the secret to great kissing is variety. According to his book, there are at least thirty ways to do it. "Don't just do French kisses," Cane says. "Try lip kisses, neck and ear kisses, sliding and upside-down kisses, lip-o-suction, biting kisses and any others your imagination can devise on the spur of the moment."

Is kissing overrated? Not when you've mastered Cane's "candy kiss," "electric kiss," and "Trobriand Islands kiss." This last one may involve biting, bleeding, hair-pulling, and eyebrow nibbling, depending on how far you wish to take it.

If you need a visual aid, *The Art of Kissing* is available as an instructional DVD. This video promises to show you "how to kiss like the sexiest person alive"—and it ships discreetly in plain packaging. But before you get too excited, know that *The Art of Kissing* is billed as "PG-rated material" and the "perfect gift for teens." How's that for overrated?

Q Do men ever say, "Not tonight, dear, I have a headache"?

A If you had your choice of having lunch or not having lunch, which would you choose? Lunch, right? Well to guys, sex is like that lunch. Why skip it when you could just as easily make a tasty bologna sandwich? Everything you need is right there waiting for you in the fridge.

Mustard and sweet pickles aside, this probably comes as no surprise. No doubt you've heard the amazing statistics: Men think about sex every seven seconds, right? Well, that's a bit of an over-statement. But they're definitely thinking about sex more often than females are.

According to The Kinsey Institute for Research in Sex, Gender, and Reproduction, 54 percent of men think about sex every day, or several times a day. In comparison, only 19 percent of women think about sex every day. The majority of women, 67 percent, cop to a sexual fantasy just a few times per month. The remaining 14 percent of women think about sex even less frequently than that.

The result? It's pretty common for couples to experience discrep-ancies in sexual desire. Studies reveal that half of all married men say that their wives have turned them down for sex, according to marriage therapist Richard Driscoll. In contrast, only one in five women say that their husbands have turned them down.

So why are the ladies holding out? Scientists blame biology. Turns out, women may be hardwired to be cautious about sex because they're the ones who will wind up getting pregnant and taking care of the babies. Men, on the other hand, are programmed to disseminate their genetic material. Driscoll says that males of almost every species in the animal kingdom take a more avid interest in sex. Compared to the females, they've got everything to gain—and not much to lose.

Even with the advent of condoms, IUDs, and birth control pills and patches, differences in sexual desire seem to remain driven by evolutionary forces. Researchers at Germany's Hamburg-

Eppendorf University Hospital have found that a man's libido tends to hold steady over the course of a relationship, no matter how long he's in it. But a woman's libido begins to take a deep dive after just four years.

Researchers explain that women have evolved to have a high sex drive at the beginning of a relationship so as to facilitate a pair bond with their partner. But once that bond is established and secure, women become less and less interested in sex.

So, guys, the next time your wife rolls over and plays dead in bed, don't take it personally. In fact, it just may be that she really does have a headache. Three out of four migraine suffers are women. Go get her an Excedrin, and while you're at it, take out the trash and do the dishes. That just might be enough to get you a tasty bologna sandwich tomorrow.

Q Why did women start wearing high heels?

A "High heels were invented by a woman who had been kissed on the forehead," quipped twentieth-century American writer Christopher Morley. He may have been on to something.

Though the precise history of the high heel is somewhat up in the air, it's believed that the first woman to strut in stilettos was a particularly petite gal named Catherine de Medici. Yes, that Catherine de Medici. In 1533, this member of the influential Italian Renaissance family commissioned a Florentine artist to craft a very special pair of shoes for her forthcoming nuptials to Henry, the rather tall duke of Orleans and the son of France's King Francis I.

Like any bride, Catherine wanted to make a grand entrance at her wedding. But impressing the Royal Court of France was a pretty tall order for a girl who was less than five feet tall. That she was merely fourteen years old perhaps added to the pressure.

The Italian artisan consulted by Catherine came through with the perfect pair of shoes to temporarily elevate her stature. Indeed, upon arriving in France, Catherine's higher heels caused quite the stir among the ladies of the French court. They were, at once, *en vogue* and went on to become a fashion staple.

Today, designer heels from such names as Jimmy Choo, Stuart Weitzman, and Christian Louboutin are essential to the with-it woman's accessory arsenal. They make her look taller and pro- mote the illusion of slender, toned legs. And wearing high heels also pushes the chest forward and the butt rearward, accentuat- ing the feminine form—or, at least, the male ideal of the feminine form.

Most women will confess is that while high heels look good, darn, they hurt. Got blisters, corns, hammertoes, or bunions to go along with those sexy spikes? Curse Catherine de Medici. You'd be in fashionable company; the French never really liked the little squirt, anyway.

Chapter Five

ANIMAL KINGDOM

Q Are there really alligators in New York City sewers?

A What might be the definitive urban legend goes like this: Back in the early twentieth century, some denizens of Gotham thought that baby alligators made great gifts for kids. Apparently, these knuckleheads couldn't foresee that cute baby alligators would become ugly, adult limb-manglers.

When the gators grew and became dangerous, these New Yorkers flushed the animals into the city's sewer system. There, these warm-climate amphibians found a friendly enough environment, and abandoned alligators, it was said, formed a thriving colony beneath the Manhattan streets.

Fueling the legend was Robert Daley's 1959 book *The World Beneath the City*. According to the book, Teddy May, a former sewer superintendent, claimed that in the 1930s he saw gators as long as two feet in the sewer tunnels. May said that he ordered his charges to kill the reptiles and that it took a few months to complete the job.

Indeed, the 1930s were a golden age for news stories of alligator sightings in and around the city. Oddly, accounts involving the sewer system were rare. Most reports involved surface-level encounters, and the critters in question are believed to have been escaped pets. A February 1935 article in the *New York Times* told of a group of boys who discovered that the manhole into which they were shoveling snow contained an alligator. They used a clothesline to drag the reptile up to the street, then beat it to death with their shovels. Welcome to the Big Apple.

Curiously, no contemporary news coverage of Teddy May's extended alligator hunt can be found. Subsequent published reports painted May as a bit of a raconteur who quite possibly was having some fun at the expense of author Daley. We're not saying you won't encounter some sort of underground wildlife in NYC, but you're more likely to find it on the subway than in the sewers.

Q Why are black cats considered bad luck?

A In some places, actually, black cats are considered *good* luck. Such as England, where they've been given credit for victory on the soccer field and success on the hunt. And an old Scottish proverb claims that black cats have a romantic influence as well—supposedly, if you have one in the house, your daughters will have plenty of boyfriends. (We'll let you decide whether this is good or back luck.)

Whichever way the luck winds up going, black cats have been the objects of superstition, worship, and dread for thousands of years. In ancient Egypt, where cats were first domesticated, there was a cult that worshipped a cat-goddess called Bastet. She was usually represented with a womanlike body and a feline head, and to the believers, she was both a loving maternal figure and a terrifying punisher. One ancient historian claimed that a yearly festival devoted to Bastet attracted hundreds of thousands of Egyptians. People arrived at the festival by riverboat, playing music, drinking heroic amounts of wine, and "displaying themselves" to anyone who happened to be standing by the side of the river. (Apparently ancient history had a lot in common with *Girls Gone Wild.*)

Unfortunately, though, there's always someone who wants to ruin a good time. And for these hard-partying folks, it turned out that Christianity was the ultimate buzz-kill. As paganism died out, cats became more and more unpopular; eventually, they were thought to be servants of the Devil himself. In medieval times, church enforcers targeted Christian heretics—people like the Knights Templar, who were outside the mainstream of Christianity—and tortured them into confessing (among other things) that they worshipped a giant black cat and literally kissed its butt. At the time, this was thought to be a sure sign of Satanism, though we know of many cats today that manage to put their owners in a similar position.

Eventually, cats—especially black cats—came to be associated with witches. They were often thought to be either embodiments of the Devil or demonic servants that would do the bidding of witches. Because of this unfortunate association, cats were treated with incredible cruelty. It was common for them to be dropped into boiling water, hurled from the tops of church towers, burned alive in festive holiday bonfires, and used as targets to practice archery. The belief that black cats are bad luck was firmly established during this era of barbaric treatment.

Happily, black cats have, by and large, become respectable once again. But considering what the breed has been through over the years, it may be a good idea, the next time one crosses your path, to stop worrying about your luck and just give it a loving pat on the head.

Q Why do dogs lick people?

A When a dog licks your face, it feels kind of like you're being kissed. And according to the most popular theory related to dog licking, that perception isn't far from the truth.

One reason dogs lick is to show affection. Like a kiss hello between two good friends, a few licks on the hand or the face express how the canine feels about the person in its life. Just like we humans, some dogs are more affectionate than others. A dog's personality and age can influence how openly it licks—an excitable young pup is apt to be more forthcoming with its affection than a stately older dog. Dog experts say that licking is basically a social activity. For example, puppies lick each other as displays of affection and to groom each other; they'll lick their mothers to indicate that they're ready to feed.

So a dog's tongue on your skin can mean a couple of things: Fido might want some love, or some food. If those licks turn to nibbles, you'll know that it's the latter.

Q Are some bookworms really worms?

A Librarians hate bookworms. They'd like to banish them from the stacks forever. The literature lovers in question aren't people—they're tiny winged creatures known as book lice or barklice. They resemble flies, not worms, and they don't even like paper. They feed off mold and usually are found in damp, mildewed tomes.

Other bugs, including silverfish and cockroaches, feast on organic substances such as the flour and cornstarch found in old library paste. Wood-boring beetles eat wood, naturally, but will consume paper made of wood pulp, too. Though beetles technically are not worms, they probably inspired the term "bookworm."

Nineteenth-century French book dealer and bibliophile Étienne-Gabriel Peignot reported finding a bookworm that had burrowed clear through a set of twenty-seven volumes, leaving a single hole, like the track of a bullet, in its wake. How far did it go? Given that many old tomes are at least three inches thick, the critter might have traveled nearly seven feet.

The best way to keep bugs out of books is to stop them before they get in. Contemporary librarians strive to maintain clean, dry buildings. Replacing wood shelving with metal discourages beetles. And those signs that say, "Please do not eat in the stacks"? Heed them. A few moldy crumbs can be a bonanza to hungry book lice. Once insects settle in, it's difficult to get rid of them. Sometimes the only effective method is professional fumigation.

Modern construction and bookbinding methods have done a lot to make libraries free of bookworms—free of the six-legged kind, that is. If you're a human bookworm, come right in. Just check your lunch at the door.

Q Did Saint Bernards really rescue people in the Alps?

A Absolutely. In fact, they've rescued about two thousand people since the early eighteenth century. One Saint Bernard named Barry is credited with saving forty lives in the snowy Alps.

The dogs were trained to work in the dangerous Grand-St-Bernard Pass, an ancient route through the Swiss Alps. The eight-thousand-foot-high pass was plagued by deep snow and avalanches, and by thieves who preyed on travelers. Still, the pass was heavily traveled for centuries by farmers and merchants and by the Romans, Huns, and Hannibal's army.

In the tenth century, a priest named Bernard of Menthon came up with the idea of building a hospice on the pass to shelter travelers. After he died, Bernard became Saint Bernard, patron saint of the Alps.

What about the dogs? The hospice was isolated, so dogs from the valleys were brought up and trained. The breed we call Saint Bernard was common to the region's villages and farms. These dogs were huge and hearty. No one knows when they were first brought to the hospice; the original building and its archives burned in the fifteen hundreds. The hospice was rebuilt, and a 1707 record mentions a dog lost in an avalanche.

From the time of Bernard of Menthon, the monks at the hospice rescued and tended to travelers. Adding dogs was a smart move. Their powerful bodies plowed through snow faster than men could, their noses sniffed out lost travelers, and they had an uncanny ability to find safe passage through the terrain. The dogs made excellent guards, guides, pathfinders, and companions. Contrary to legend, they didn't have little barrels of brandy hanging from their collars. But the dogs would stretch across people they dug out of the snow to warm their bodies, and lick their faces.

Tunnels, roads, and rail lines built in the twentieth century bypass the Saint Bernard hospice, so the pass is not used much anymore—the last documented rescue was in 1897. Only four monks now live at the Saint Bernard hospice. In 2004, the hospice made headlines around the world when the monks offered their dogs for sale, with the stipulation that the new owners bring them back to the hospice each year for a visit.

Q Why don't animals need glasses?

A Humans are so quick to jump to conclusions. Just because you've never sat next to an orangutan at the optometrist's office or seen a cat adjust its contact lenses, you assume that animals don't need corrective eyewear.

Animals do develop myopia (nearsightedness), though it seems less widespread in nature than among humans. For one thing, nearsighted animals—especially carnivores—would have an extremely difficult time hunting in the wild. As dictated by the rules of natural selection, animals carrying the myopia gene would die out and, thus, wouldn't pass on the defective gene.

For years, nearsightedness was thought to be mainly hereditary, but relatively recent studies have shown that other factors may also contribute to the development of myopia. Some researchers have suggested that myopia is rare in illiterate societies and that it increases as societies become more educated. This doesn't mean that education causes nearsightedness, but some scientists have speculated that reading and other "close work" can play a role in the development of the condition.

In accordance with this theory, a study of the Inuit in Barrow, Alaska, conducted in the 1960s found that myopia was much more common in younger people than in older generations, perhaps coinciding with the introduction of schooling and mass literacy in Inuit culture that had recently occurred. But schooling was just one component of a larger shift—from the harsh, traditional lifestyle of hunting and fishing at the edge of the world to a more modern, Western lifestyle. Some scientists believe that the increase of myopia was actually due to other changes that went along with this shift, such as the switch from eating primarily fish and seal meat to a more Western diet. This diet is heavier on processed grains, which, some experts believe, can have a bad influence on eye development.

And this brings us back to animals. Your beloved Fido subsists on ready-made kibble that's heavy on processed grains, but its ancient ancestors at raw flesh. If this switch to processed grains might have a negative effect on the eyesight of humans, why not in animals, too?

Unfortunately, there's not much we can do for a nearsighted animal. Corrective lenses are impractical, glasses would fall off, and laser surgery is just too darn expensive. Sorry, Fido!

Q Why do cats always land on their feet?

A It's true: Cats have an uncanny ability to survive a fall. Maybe that's why we say they have nine lives. However, the notion that they always land on their feet isn't exactly accurate.

Every once in a while, a cat does indeed go splat. And it's probably because a very sorry owner left a window or balcony door open.

Cats are not afraid of heights. If they see a tasty bird or butterfly floating about outside, their predatory instincts kick in and it's jump time. This phenomenon is so common that a 1987 study of falling cats in the *Journal of the American Veterinary Medical Association* even gave it a name: High-Rise Syndrome. New York City veterinarians often use the term to describe the injuries that cats sustain after falling from the city's high-rise apartment windows.

Whether a cat lands on its feet after a fall depends on several factors, including the distance it plummets and the surface on which it lands. If a cat falls a short distance (say, fewer than one or two stories), it usually can right itself in midair. How? For starters, cats have an amazing sense of balance and coordination. Each of their inner ears is outfitted with a vestibular apparatus, a tiny fluid-filled organ that helps them register which way is up. When the cat is falling, the fluid in the inner ear shifts, telling the cat to reorient its head until the fluid is once again equalized and level.

When a cat turns its head and forefeet, the rest of its body naturally follows. How so? Cats have super-flexible musculoskeletal systems. A cat's backbone is like a universal joint—it has thirty vertebrae (five more than a human) and no collarbone. This is why cats are so agile. With this freedom of movement, a cat can instantly bend and rotate like a pretzel to land on its feet.

If a cat falls from more than one or two stories, it likely will sustain severe or fatal injuries, even if it can right itself. Its legs and feet simply cannot absorb all the shock. That said, the study in the *Journal of the American Veterinary Medical Association* revealed something really surprising: Of the 132 high-rise cats that veterinarians examined, those that fell from above seven stories had a better chance of escaping injury.

It seems that after plummeting five stories or so, cats reach a nonfatal terminal falling velocity; at this point, they are able to relax their muscles and spread their bodies out like feline parachutes or flying squirrels, and they arch their backs just before hitting bottom, reducing the force of the impact. Just how far can a cat fall without being killed? The longest nonfatal fall on record is forty-two floors.

Q Why is my dog eating grass?

A Strange as it may seem, this behavior is perfectly natural. You know how you supplement your porterhouse with a salad when you're at your favorite steak joint? A dog is doing essentially the same thing—a side of greens can really round out a meal.

The most widely accepted theory among veterinarians is that Fido's ancestors inadvertently consumed greens with almost every meal. The animals they hunted were mostly herbivores and had bellyfuls of berries, barks, and grasses. Today's dogs, then, are hardwired to crave greens (i.e., your lawn).

Some dog owners believe that their pooches chow down on grass to induce vomiting, as one often precedes the other, but veterinarians generally dismiss of this explanation. And let's face it: The notion that dogs use plants for medicinal purposes, such as soothing an upset stomach, seems a bit far-fetched. It's more likely that certain chemicals, such as an insecticide or a fertilizer, cause the vomiting.

Of course, dogs may eat grass simply because they like it. The grass is there, it smells good, the dog's hungry—why not have a few bites?

Q Why do zebras have stripes?

A The zebra is among the flashy few of the animal world. Like the butterfly, the tiger, and the peacock, the zebra looks like it treated itself to a vanity paint job. Which is why one of the theories explaining the evolutionary advantage of those flamboyant stripes sounds counter-intuitive: The stripes may actually help zebras blend in.

For one thing, vertical stripes can mesh pretty well with the vertical lines made by the tall grass that covers the ground in much of the zebra's natural habitat. There's a noticeable color difference, of course—tall grass comes in shades of yellow, green, and brown that don't exactly match the zebra's stark black-and-white coat. But this probably doesn't matter much, since the zebra's primary predators—the lion and hyena—seem to be colorblind.

The stripes may also provide the zebras with another way to visually confuse their predators. Zebras usually stick together in herds, where the clusters of vertical stripes can make it tricky for predators to figure out where one zebra ends and the other zebra begins. A lion, for example, might have difficulty homing in on any specific zebra, especially the more vulnerable foals. And once the herd starts to move, it's just a blur of stripes.

Some zoologists don't put much stock in the camouflage theory and suggest that the real evolutionary advantage of stripes has to do with a zebra's social life. Every zebra has a unique stripe pattern that can allow the animal to easily identify a friend (or perhaps a mortal enemy). Each zebra's stripe pattern serves as a sort of name tag, a way to be identified within a massive herd. Stripes may also help zebras stick together when predators attack, even at night. In case of emergency, zebra logic may say, follow the stripes.

Another theory suggests that zebra stripes are really a type of bug repellent. Tsetse flies, like other parasitic biting arthropods, seem to be drawn to large, one-colored surfaces—after all, that's how most large animals can be identified. But zebra stripes defy the norm, which may cause the tsetse flies to overlook the beasts when they're hunting for a free meal. There's strong evidence to support this theory: First, tsetse flies bite zebras much less frequently than they do other big animals. Second, there are more tsetse flies in the regions of Africa where zebras sport more pronounced patterns of stripes.

Of course, it's possible that the stripes may serve all of these purposes, at least to some degree. Or perhaps zebras are simply showing off.

Q Why do we never see baby pigeons?

A If you aren't seeing baby pigeons, you're just looking in the wrong places. Until they're ready to take flight, the young birds hang out in nests while their moms and dads are out socializing.

Pigeons, those head-bobbing city slickers that so often repaint statues and other objects of their "affection," are descended from rock doves, which got their name from their propensity for building their nests on the craggy faces of cliffs. When the rock dove population spills into a metropolitan area—or when the ever-expanding metropolitan area infringes on rock dove territory—the birds build their nests on the unnatural ledges and shelves of tall buildings and bridges.

Baby pigeons, known as squabs, stay in their nests until they are able to fly. Obviously, squabs are as common as adult pigeons. They're just not as visible—unless you're a window washer.

Q Why do some animals have horns?

A Ever locked horns with someone? Unless you have a very unusual skull, you were only butting heads metaphorically. (We hope.) But male deer literally do lock horns in annual head-butting contests, which determine the buck that will win the affections of the fertile does. Each buck tries to force its opponent's head lower. On rare occasions, their antlers become so thoroughly interlocked that they cannot separate; they eventually starve to death together. It's a high price to pay for a little showing off.

Although antlers can be used to deter predators, zoologists believe that their main purpose is to impress the opposite sex. Among deer, an elaborate set of antlers is a way of saying, "I've got great genes!"

Technically, antlers and horns, both of which are composed of bone, are not quite the same thing. True horns—which are found on bovines, such as sheep, goats, and cattle—are coated with keratin, the same protein substance that forms human finger-nails and animal hoofs. They appear on both males and females, though male horns are usually larger. Horns come in a variety of shapes—straight, curved, curled, twisted, or spiraled—but they are not branched like antlers. If broken, they cannot regenerate.

Horns on domestic animals are often blunted or filed down by their owners to prevent the animals from hurting themselves or others. Because most livestock breeding is accomplished by artificial insemination these days, head-butting competitions are a thing of the past on the ranch, and horns are an evolutionary adaptation that is no longer needed.

Antlers belong to beasts from the *cervidae* family, which includes deer, elk, caribou, and moose. Unlike horns, antlers are not cov-ered by keratin, and they are shed every year in the winter; they regenerate in the spring. Only males have antlers, with the excep-tion of caribou. Females of this species sport antlers, too (leading some "Santa-ologists" to suspect that Rudolph the Red-Nosed Reindeer may have actually been a girl).

Most antlers are sharp and multipronged—the better with which to fight. The spoon-shaped, or palmated, antlers of moose, however, do double duty as hearing aids. A particularly good set of antlers can boost a male moose's hearing nearly 20 percent by funneling sound toward the ear. Since moose tend to be solitary creatures, this can be a distinct advantage in locating potential mates.

What about other "horned" animals? The narwhal whale has a long tusk that sometimes appears to be a horn, though it is actually formed from the same material as teeth. Horned lizards have bony projections on their heads and spine that they use for defense; they inflate themselves, forming a spiny balloon that protects them from predators.

Rhinoceros horns are composed entirely of keratin, with no bone at all. These horns are unique among mammals because they sit not atop the head, but on the forehead and above the nose. Full-grown rhinos have few predators, but they can use their horns to defend their young and, of course, to attract romance—proving once more that beauty is in the eye of the beholder.

Q Why doesn't a poisonous creature get killed by its own venom?

A Before we get carried away, it's only right to point out the difference between venomous and poisonous creatures. Venomous creatures—such as certain snakes, scorpions, and spiders—produce poison and have developed ways of delivering it (fangs, stingers, etc.). Poisonous creatures—such as dart frogs—also produce poison but have no way of getting it into the bloodstream of the intended victim; the prey has to ingest it.

For the sake of simplicity, we'll focus on the venomous variety. A logical assumption is that all of these creatures have developed immunities to their own toxins, but that's not entirely true. If a snake accidentally bites itself and releases its venom into its body, it will die.

Indeed, the only things that keep the poison in check are the glands that store the poison. You see, these creatures produce venom in special sacs, which are connected to their puncturing tools. These sacs have linings that prevent the venom from escaping to the rest of the creature's body. The sacs aren't unlike your own stomach, which produces all sorts of powerful acids and toxins that would eat you from the inside out if you didn't have a protective stomach lining.

Q Why don't birds fall when they sleep on a tree limb?

A No matter where you live, birds are likely to be a part of the landscape. They eat from the feeder in your yard, beg for food in the park, hop along on the ground, build nests and care for their chicks, and poop on your car (or on you, if you're unlucky). But you probably aren't as likely to see birds in one of their most vulnerable states: sleeping.

Nest-building birds don't sleep in nests; they just use them to raise their families. Some birds crouch down in the grass or in bushes to get some shuteye. However, there are many species of birds that sleep while perched on tree limbs. It seems impossible that they could stay up in a tree while asleep—after all, when people (as well as many other animals) fall asleep, they usually go limp. But perching birds, or passerines, are different, and it's all because of their feet.

Most birds have four toes on each foot, and these toes can be arranged in different configurations depending on the bird. A passerine typically has an anisodactyl foot, which consists of three toes that face forward and a "big toe," or a hallux, that faces backward. This type of bird possesses an ingenious tendon-locking mechanism (TLM) that causes a special ligament in the back of the leg to tighten automatically when the bird sits on a limb.

This tendon locks the toes and secures the bird onto the perch. Because of the TLM, a bird doesn't have to keep its muscles actively engaged to maintain its grip. The bird stays on the limb until it retracts its toes. Other animals—bats, for example—have a similar mechanism to allow them to hang upside down without falling.

On a morbid note, the TLM doesn't disengage when a bird dies, either. Skeletons have been found still perched in the trees that the birds chose when they went to sleep. So when a bird clamps down for the night, it could be for eternal sleep instead of just a night's worth.

Q Why do riders mount horses from the left?

A Riders have mounted their faithful steeds from the left for thousands of years—basically, ever since the horse was domesticated. Some things have changed since those early days: The popularization of stirrups circa AD 400, for example, made mounting much easier, since you no longer had to yank yourself up using a handful of mane. But mounting horses from the left continues, mostly out of tradition.

As for how the tradition started, it all comes down to the sword. Back when we used to settle our differences with pointy metal things, a man would typically wear his sword on his left side and draw it with his right hand for easy and agile slashing. If he had a sword hanging from his left hip, he had to get on his horse from the left, too—otherwise the sword would hit or brush up against the horse's backside, which could startle the horse and leave the rider in the dust.

Xenophon, an ancient Greek adventurer who was a (rather dull) pupil of Socrates, suggested in his treatise on horsemanship that horses be trained to accept a rider from either side, since it's imperative in a battle that you be able to get out of Dodge at a moment's notice. Evidently, no one listened to Xenophon.

Even though few people who mount horses these days are wearing swords, it's still important to have an accepted, standard side. Horses are wired to think of themselves as prey; they're always on the lookout for a lion, even on a dude ranch in Texas. Because of this, they're wary of anything approaching them from the sides. Horses need to be conditioned to feel comfortable being mounted from the side—and there's no good reason not to stick with the left. Without a uniform side, a rider would have to guess whether the horse had been trained from the left or right; there would be a 50 percent chance of sending the steed into a body-bashing tizzy

If you always remember to mount a horse from the left, it should be happy trails. Unless a lion is nearby.

Q Why do dead animals' legs sometimes stick straight up in the air?

A Contrary to what you saw on television on Saturday mornings as a kid, they don't. Typically, a dead animal's legs stick wherever they were pointing when it died. There are some exceptions—the spider, for instance—but it's really only in cartoons that animals die on their backs, their limbs thrusting skyward.

It's possible that the idea for this awkward pose came from observing the effects of rigor mortis. When an animal dies, the biochemical reactions that allow its muscles to move suddenly cease. The main player is adenosine triphosphate (ATP), an energy-carrying molecule that the body constantly synthesizes. To create ATP, the muscle tissue needs oxygen; when an animal stops breathing, the ATP supply rapidly dwindles.

Without ATP, the fibers that make up the muscle tissue become locked together. After a few hours, the muscles freeze up, and they remain this way for two or three days before the muscle cells begin breaking down and their contents drain out. At this point, the body becomes flexible again.

Strychnic poisoning could be another inspiration for the cartoonish depictions of animals dying. A typical cartoon death is characterized by the sudden, spastic extension of the legs, followed immediately by the rigidity of full-on rigor mortis.

The effects of strychnic poisoning, according to *Lewis' Dictionary of Toxicology,* are similar to this: A person who has been dosed with strychnine will suddenly extend his arms and legs, turn his toes inward, and die of suffocation when his lungs seize up. Still, such a fate isn't really within the realm of possibility in the animal kingdom. Animals in the wild don't often get poisoned, and when they do, it's usually not with strychnine.

Let this serve as an illustration of how our view of the world is formed early in life. Bugs and Daffy have taught us much— problem is, little of it stands up to scrutiny.

Q Why do bees die after they sting?

A You're out in the yard on summer day, pulling weeds in the garden, flipping burgers on the grill, or lounging in the shade. Suddenly, you feel the sharp tip of a bee's stinger in your skin. What did you possibly do to deserve it? Sure, it's just a bee sting, but it hurts! While you are still smarting from this unprovoked attack and are cursing all of the insects on the planet, you can take consolation in the notion that the bee might have given up its life when it recklessly chose to sting you. We really should explain that.

First, it depends on the type of bee that stung you. Only honey-bees die after stinging. The honeybee has a large barb on its sting-er; when the bee stings, the barb usually catches in the victim's skin. (This only happens when a honeybee stings a victim pos-sessing elastic-like skin that can entangle the barb, like a human. If the barb doesn't get caught, the honeybee can fly off to sting another day.) As the stuck honeybee tries to dislodge its stinger, it usually tears its abdomen, along with muscles and nerves, caus-ing the insect to die within a few minutes.

The honeybees that sting are always females and are known as worker bees. The queen bee is the only sexually mature female in a colony and the only one capable of laying eggs. Instead of having an ovipositor (egg-laying organ) like the queen, a worker has a barb. When a worker bee perceives a threat to itself or to the hive, it stings. A typical hive has thousands and thousands of workers, so a few lost on occasion hardly matters. You might say that it's a job to die for.

Q Who determines which species are endangered?

A What do the Indiana bat, the San Francisco garter snake, and the Hawaiian dark-rumped petrel have in common? They all appeared on the first list of endangered species issued by the U.S. Fish and Wildlife Service (USFWS) in 1966. The list, compiled by nine biologists from the department's Committee on Rare and Endangered Wildlife Species, was at least in part the government's response to the furor sparked by Rachel Carson's 1962 book *Silent Spring,* which examined the impact of pesticides on the environment.

The Endangered Species Act of 1973 widened the scope of the USFWS's power, giving the federal government the authority to protect the habitats of endangered species from development, whether or not those habitats rested on public lands. Meanwhile, on a global level, the International Union for the Conservation of Nature (IUCN) had released its own list in 1962, the Red List of Threatened Species. Based on research conducted by the multinational Species Survival Commission, this list inspired the 1963 formation of the Convention on International Trade in Endangered Species of Wild Flora and Fauna.

By the end of the twentieth century, environmentalism had become a major movement and the phrase "endangered species" was part every school kid's vocabulary. But what does "endangered" mean? How many of a species have to die off before the remaining ones are considered endangered? Obviously, numbers alone don't tell the entire story. First, it can be hard to count individual members of a species in the wild. Second, it's difficult to compare the populations of small life-forms with those of larger ones. Ten thousand pomace flies can be just as endangered as ten polar bears, though hardly as photogenic.

The criteria used by the IUCN to determine whether a species is endangered include decrease in total population, decrease in the range of habitat, and probability of extinction. The population of the western lowland gorilla, for instance, has declined more than 60 percent since the 1980s due to poaching, disease, and the loss of portions of its habitat. This combination of misfortunes has placed the animal high in the IUCN's critically endangered category. Species with this designation have a 50 percent chance of becoming extinct within ten years or during three generations, whichever is longer, if a major effort is not made to preserve them.

As of 2007, the IUCN had listed 16,306 endangered species worldwide and another 41,415 as threatened though not yet endangered. The USFWS listed 448 animals and 598 plants as endangered in the United States. Together, these two organizations provide us with a fairly accurate assessment of which species are at the greatest risk of being lost forever.

As for our old friends the Indiana bat, the San Francisco garter snake, and the Hawaiian dark-rumped petrel? They're still hanging in there. Not yet out of danger—but thanks to the work of environmentalists, not extinct either.

Chapter Six

SPORTS

Q **What's up with the scoring system in tennis?**

A The British are an odd bunch. They call trucks "lorries," drugstores "chemists," and telephones "blowers." They put meat in pies, celebrate a holiday called Boxing Day that has nothing to do with boxing, and eat something called "spotted dick." So it shouldn't be surprising that tennis, one of Britain's national pastimes, has such a bizarre scoring system.

For those who haven't been to the tennis club lately, here's a refresher on how scoring works. The first player to four points is the winner of the match, but points are not counted by one, two, six, or any other logical number—they go by fifteen for the first two points of the game, then ten for the third point. The sequence, then, is: 0–15–30–40. Except it's not zero—it's called "love." So: love–15–30–40. To confuse matters further, if both players are tied at forty, it's not a tie—it's called "deuce." Say what? Just trying to figure out this scoring system makes one long for a gin gimlet and a cold compress.

Gin gimlets, in fact, may have been the order of the day when modern tennis was invented. According to most tennis historians, it dates back to the early 1870s, when the delightfully named Major Walter Clopton Wingfield devised a lawn game for the entertainment of party guests on his English country estate. Wingfield (whose bust graces the Wimbledon Tennis Museum) based his game on an older form of tennis that long had been popular in France and England, called "real tennis."

Unfortunately, the origin of tennis' odd scoring system is as obfuscated as the system itself. A number of historians argue that Wingfield, being somewhat of a pompous ass, borrowed the terms for his new game from the older French version, even though they made no sense once adapted into English. Hence, l'oeuf (meaning "egg") turned into "love." And a deux le jeu ("to two the game") became "deuce."

Furthermore, Wingfield opted to borrow the counting system from earlier versions of tennis—in French, scoring mimicked the quarter-hours of the clock: 15–30–45. For some unknown reason (possibly too many gin gimlets), 45 became 40, and we have the scoring system that we know and love (no pun intended) today.

There are plenty of other theories about where the scoring system originated, including "love" coming from the Flemish lof (meaning "honor") and "deuce" originating in ancient card games. Others argue that scoring by fifteen was based on the value of the *sou,* a medieval French coin. However, in the absence of definitive evidence, we prefer to attribute the ludicrous scoring system to drunken Brits.

Q Can a male have a sex change and play in the WNBA?

A The average guy watching the WNBA, a women's pro basketball league, might think: "*I* could play better than this!" With recent advances in medical technology, and perhaps with the aid of a few malted-barley beverages, it might not take long for said average guy to wonder whether it would be possible to have a sex change in order to go on to fame and fortune in the WNBA. And it's not just average guys who would consider this—former Seattle SuperSonics point guard Gary Payton once famously stated that for a hundred million dollars, he'd undergo a sex change to play in the WNBA. (Sorry, Gary, the average WNBA salary is about fifty grand.)

We have good news and bad news for male WNBA dreamers: There is nothing explicitly stated in the rulebook that prohibits a transsexual (a man who has had a sex-change operation) from participating in the WNBA. This stands in contrast to the Ladies Professional Golf Association, which has a "female at birth" clause that prohibits transsexuals from playing on tour. However, other sports organizations are getting with the inclusive times. The Ladies European Tour recently changed its rules to allow transsexuals to participate in its Europe-based golf events, and the

International Association of Athletics Federations (track and field's ruling body) also allows for it.

Even the mighty International Olympic Committee (IOC) is making the switch. The Olympics, of course, have a long and proud history of men disguising themselves as women in order to win glory. This tradition dates back to at least 1936, when German athlete Hermann Ratjen, under supposed coercion from Nazi officials, competed in the high jump under the name Dora Ratjen. (Humiliatingly, Hermann placed only fourth.) During the Cold War years, the numerous Soviet-bloc athletes who were accused of dressing in drag to win gold medals eventually led the IOC to start gender testing, a practice that lasted until 2000. But in 2004, the IOC startled the sports world by passing a resolution making transsexual athletes eligible to compete in Olympic events as members of their new sex.

So that's the good news. The bad news? Well, the whole bit about undergoing a sex-change operation.

Q Does buzkashi have any chance of becoming an Olympic sport?

A Imagine a game in which the "ball" is the carcass of a goat, decapitated, dehoofed, and soaked overnight in cold water to make it stiff. The players are mounted on horseback and wear traditional Uzbek garb: turbans, robes, and scarves around their waists. There's no complicated playbook, only a minimally regimented strategy that requires—encourages—no-holds-barred violence. The referees carry rifles, in case things really get out of hand. The field has no set boundaries; spectators are in constant danger of being trampled. The objective is to gain possession of the goat and carry it to a designated goal. And the winning players cook and eat the carcass.

This is buzkashi, the national sport of Afghanistan. Buzkashi translates to "goat pulling" and likely evolved from ordinary herding. It originated with nomadic Turkic peoples who moved west from China and Mongolia from the tenth to fifteenth centuries. Today, it's played mainly in Afghanistan, but you can also find folks yanking the ol' carcass in northwestern China and in the Muslim republics north of Afghanistan.

The game has two basic forms: modern and traditional. The modern involves teams of ten to twelve riders. In the traditional form, it's every man for himself. Both require a combination of strength and expert horsemanship. The best players are generally over the age of forty, and their mounts are trained for up to five years before entering a match.

There's typically more at stake in a tournament than a tasty repast of pulled goat. The competitions often are sponsored by *khans* ("traditional elites") who gain or lose status based on the success of the events. And in this case, success is defined by how little or how much mayhem erupts. Biting, hair-pulling, grabbing another rider's reins, and using weapons is prohibited in buzkashi. Anything else goes.

Could it become an Olympic sport?

Don't count on it. Then again, in a world in which millions of people tune in each week to watch socially inept twenty-somethings eat insects for fun, fame, and prizes, is barbarous goat-pulling all that far-fetched?

Q Is the gambling industry rigged in favor of the house?

A Remember those ads that said, "What Happens in Vegas Stays in Vegas"? The ones that seemed to suggest that there are hordes of jaw-droppingly beautiful women who can't wait to get to Sin City and copulate with complete strangers? Here's a little secret for you: Those advertisements may not have been 100 percent accurate.

You see, the folks who own the casinos in Las Vegas are always looking for ways to lure you there. Because they know that once you arrive and figure out that the horny-supermodel quotient isn't nearly as high as the creepy-guys-looking-for-horny-supermodels quotient (not to mention the chain-smoking-senior-citizen quotient), you'll shrug your shoulders and find something else to do. Namely, gambling. And then they've got you. The beauty of Las Vegas (and we mean the beauty from the casino owners' perspective, not the stunning beauty of the fake Eiffel Tower or the fake Venetian canals) is that the games don't have to be *rigged* in favor of the house—they're set up in favor of the house, *openly* and *legally.*

Casino owners carefully study the probable outcomes of their games and then design the rules so that the house will win a certain small percentage over the long haul. Government bodies like the Nevada Gaming Commission regulate these house advantages and work to ensure that the casinos stick to them. If the house advantage on a game is 5 percent, that means the casino will pocket about 5 percent of all the money gambled, returning the other 95 percent to the players. But the returned money is distributed unequally—many gamblers will have small losses or gains while a few will win (or lose) big. And the possibility of becoming a big winner is what keeps you going, in spite of the fact that in the long term, when all things are considered, the house always wins.

The percentages vary by game, but they can exceed 10 percent in some cases. If you study the rules of blackjack, for example, and learn how to play it skillfully, you'll have better odds of winning than if you drop all your dough into a slot machine, which is typically your worst bet. Nevertheless, even blackjack favors the house.

So, yes, the gambling industry is set up so that the casino owner makes a profit. What, you thought fake Eiffel Towers grow on trees?

Q How do corked bats help cheating baseball players hit the ball farther?

A In this age of performance-enhancing drugs, it's almost refreshing when a hitter gets caught cheating the old-fashioned way. Corked bats somehow recall a more innocent time.

There are different ways to cork a wooden baseball bat, but the basic procedure goes like this: Drill a hole into the top of the bat, about an inch in diameter and twelve inches deep; fill the hole with cork—in rolled sheets or ground up—and close the top with a wooden plug that matches the bat; finally, stain and finish the top of the bat so that the plug blends in.

The supposed benefits of a corked bat involve weight and bat speed. Cork is lighter than wood, which enables a player to generate more speed when swinging the bat. The quicker the swing, the greater the force upon contact with the ball—and the farther that ball flies. The lighter weight allows a batter more time to evaluate a pitch, since he can make up the difference with his quicker swing; this extra time amounts to only a fraction of a second, but it can be the difference between a hit and an out at the major league level.

Following the logic we've set forth, replacing the wood in the bat with nothing at all would make for an even lighter bat and, thus, provide more of an advantage. The problem here is that an empty core would increase the likelihood that the bat would break; at the very least, it would cause a suspicious, hollow sound upon contact with the ball. The cork fills in the hollow area, and does so in a lightweight way.

Not everyone believes that a corked bat provides an advantage; some tests have indicated that the decreased bat density actually diminishes the force applied to the ball. But Dr. Robert Watts, a mechanical engineer at Tulane University who studies sports science, sees things differently. He concluded that corking a bat increases the speed of the swing by about 2.5 percent; consequently, the ball might travel an extra fifteen to twenty feet, a distance that would add numerous home runs to a player's total over the course of his career.

In any case, we haven't heard much lately about corked bats. That's because the headlines have been dominated by players who have used steroids to cork themselves.

Q What's wrong with throwing like a girl?

A Now, here's a loaded question. Feminists—and anyone who's being truly reasonable—will point out that it's condescending. And anyone who's watched a women's softball game knows that the question is based on a faulty assumption, because women who've played a lot of ball throw every bit as well as men, though generally not as powerfully due to their smaller sizes.

The Atlantic Monthly belabored this point in its own signature way several years ago, coming to this conclusion: "The crucial factor is not that males and females are put together differently but that they typically spend their early years in different ways. Little boys often learn to throw without noticing that they are throwing. Little girls are more rarely in environments that encourage them in the same way. "

But *Atlantic Monthly* didn't consider why there's such opprobrium in throwing badly in the first place. It can't be just because baseball is so central to the American male psyche—baseball's big, but not that big. We think it might have deeper, anthropological roots, stretching back to a time when throwing deadly projectiles—spears, stones, etc.—was central to sustenance and protection. Someone who threw poorly would have been a liability to the clan.

This kind of formative reality is burned into our genes; it's possible that when we see someone throw awkwardly, we feel the primal fear of shared vulnerability. And that fear is as powerful today as it was in our knuckle-dragging days. Just ask anyone who ever watched Mitch "Wild Thing" Williams pitch.

Q Why do college football coaches have armed state troopers with them on the sideline?

A A couple of state troopers are the ultimate accessories for a major-college football coach, especially in the pigskin-crazed South. No one is certain how the tradition started, but it's usually attributed to Paul "Bear" Bryant, who was a legendary coach at the University of Alabama. The story is that Bear got a trooper entourage for security in 1958 or 1959. Not to be outdone, Ralph "Shug" Jordan, coach at Auburn University, Alabama's bitter in-state rival, secured a larger posse of troopers soon after. Let the games begin.

The tradition is both ceremonial and practical. Ceremonially, the troopers represent state pride, whether at home or away. Troopers have no law enforcement authority in another state, but armed and dressed in their official garb, they can be an imposing presence on the sideline.

From a practical perspective, the troopers' chief responsibility is to provide protection. This rarely is an issue during the game, but the playing field can fill up quickly with excited and rambunctious fans once the final seconds have ticked away. It is the job of troopers to escort the coach through the chaos to midfield for the traditional handshake with the opposing coach (who also might be flanked by troopers) and then to the locker room.

This sort of security doesn't come cheap. In 2008, ten schools in Alabama each paid the state police more than thirty-eight thousand dollars for "football detail." Some troopers in other states provide coach protection at no cost, as long as the college pays for meals and travel expenses.

The practice is nearly ubiquitous among NCAA Division I-A teams in the Southeastern Conference and has also caught on with some schools in the ACC, Big East, Big 12, and Big Ten conferences. Trooper detail hasn't taken root in the West, however—the Pacific-10 Conference is explicitly opposed to the practice. Teams without trooper support generally rely on campus police for coach security.

For a trooper assigned to a coach, staying calm, cool, and collected might be the toughest part of the gig. Troopers typically are huge fans of their assigned teams, but they're expected to maintain stoic professionalism. And this is no small feat if they've just witnessed a game-winning touchdown.

Q Can you participate in wife-carrying if you're not married?

A You certainly can. Wife-carrying is a sport that, despite its name, is open to married couples and singles alike. Members of less-blissful matrimonial pairings might even suggest it as a way for single folks to preview the rigors of married life: Men struggle to achieve their goals while burdened by the dead weight of a clinging female; women have their world turned upside down and then are forced to kiss a man's ass repeatedly.

Sounds like fun, huh?

They thought so in Finland, where the sport of wife-carrying was invented using two colorful snippets of national folklore as inspiration. Finnish men, it is said, once chose their mates by stealing them from neighboring villages. And an outlaw named Rosvo-Ronkainen recruited his bandits by putting them through races in which they carried weighted sacks. This practice was synthesized into wife-carrying, an international competition that has held its world championships in Finland each year since 1995.

The rules are fairly straightforward: A man carries a woman who weighs at least 108 pounds through an obstacle course. (Women who weigh fewer than 108 pounds carry a sack weighted to make up the difference.) Whoever completes the 253.5-meter course in the quickest is the winner. The obstacles can include different surfaces (like sand or water) and objects (like fences). In previous contests, men were penalized fifteen seconds each time they dropped their women. (As far as we know, the women may very well administer other penalties, but these aren't in the rules.) In the 2009 Wife Carrying World Championships, however, the fifteen-second penalty was omitted. It's not quite as barbaric as it sounds—the woman does wear a helmet, after all.

The popularity of wife-carrying has extended to other parts of the world, including the United States and Canada, other European countries, Africa, and even China. Many of the winners from these far-flung regions eventually travel to Finland to test their mettle in the world championships.

But nobody has taken to the sport quite like the Estonians. From 1997 to 2008, Estonians won eleven world titles. And one family, the Uusorgs of Tallinn, notched seven of those crowns, with Margo claiming five and his brother Madis the other two. There are a few different carrying techniques, but the crafty Estonians introduced what has become the most popular method, known as the Estonian carry: The woman clings to the man's back with her legs straddling his neck and her face buried in his posterior.

The egalitarian Finns claim that the ultimate goal of the competition is for everyone involved to have fun, but is there any doubt about whom this whole thing is really meant to benefit? The prize for the champion is his wife's weight in beer.

Q Why does the umpire turn his backside toward the pitcher when sweeping off home plate?

A Umpires love decorum—and why not? When your job is to keep a bunch of adrenaline-fueled jocks in line, that's perfectly understandable.

In its section on cleaning home plate, the *American Legion Umpires National Tournament Manual* begins, rather pompously, with this statement: "Every gesture and motion of an umpire means something." The manual then instructs the home plate umpire to turn his back to the pitcher's mound before bending over, "as a courtesy to fans." Hey, if an ump's every gesture means something, what's the pitcher supposed to make of being mooned every inning?

There's no consensus on the exact reason that umpires clean the plate this way. Some "experts" claim that it lets the players know beyond a shadow of a doubt that time has been called. Others say that it protects the ump if a pitch gets thrown at him by mistake while he's doing the dusting. (It's better to get hit in the butt than in the head.)

As the American Legion manual suggests, it may simply be a display of courtesy to the fans. But that doesn't stop umpires from using the move for other purposes, like surreptitiously lecturing an argumentative batter or catcher. It's a way to get a point across without showing anybody up.

Not all umpires are so formal when it comes to cleaning the plate. Former big-league ump Ken Kaiser found that he could get the job done with a quick swipe of his foot. Kaiser was amused to learn that this irritated some of his more tradition-bound colleagues. "I didn't grow up expecting to hear the commissioner of baseball telling me to clean my plate," Kaiser explained in his book *Planet of the Umps*. "As long as I could see the plate, it was clean enough for me."

Chapter Seven

FOOD AND DRINK

Q Are Rocky Mountain oysters an aphrodisiac?

A For thousands of years, people from every culture have sought to inspire or enhance the act of making love. Herbs, potions, and animal parts that look like human genitalia are among the substances that people have consumed, snorted, and rubbed on themselves in the quest for an effective aphrodisiac.

Among the most obvious and primitive aphrodisiacs are the reproductive organs of animals that are considered to be especially virile. In the American West, the-hope-to-be-hot assign erotic properties to bull testicles, delicately euphemized as "Rocky Mountain oysters."

Testicles are cut from young bulls to render the ornery beasts more docile and, thus, easier to raise for food. The soft, slimy meat is considered a delicacy. Sliced, breaded, and fried, it's served up as Rocky Mountain oysters or, if you prefer, Montana tendergroins, cowboy caviar, or swinging beef.

Brave and hungry souls—some undoubtedly possessed of the urge to merge—can be found chowing down at "testicle festivals." Many say that Rocky Mountain oysters taste like chicken; others liken the flavor to fried shrimp or marine oysters; and some maintain that the only part they can taste is the breading.

As for their power to prime the love pump? The U.S. Food and Drug Administration turns a cold shower on the notion, declaring that there's no scientific proof of the effectiveness of any reputed aphrodisiac, bull-based or otherwise. But if you think that eating a longhorn's privates can help, go ahead and have a ball.

Q Is there any difference between catsup and ketchup?

A Nope. Catsup and ketchup are exactly the same—but don't try telling that to the condiment's super-fans, who can detect the tiny variations between their brands of choice and those flavor-free rip-offs that crowd the supermarket shelves.

The confusion goes back more than three hundred years, when the word first entered the English language. "Ketchup"—the preferred spelling today—appears to have originated as a phonetic spelling of a foreign term, though etymologists don't agree on its source. One esteemed food writer has claimed that it evolved from an English variation of the French *escaveche* (meaning "food in sauce") or *escabeche* and *escaveach* (Spanish and Portuguese words for a pickling sauce). But the prevailing theory today is that the word came from the East, from *ke-tsiap,* a term from the Chinese Amoy dialect, meaning roughly "brine of fish" or "fish sauce." It's possible that this word entered the English language when British and Dutch soldiers picked up the Malay language variation, *ke-cap,* in Indonesia.

Of course, the Indonesian sauce *ke-cap* had little in common with what we call ketchup today; like the Chinese *ke-tsiap,* it was a savory condiment created by pickling fish or other sea creatures in brine. (Imagine squirting some of that onto your hamburger bun!) But when the British appropriated the term in the early eighteenth century, they used it as a catchall for many kinds of sauce. Early versions generally included anchovies or other fish, along with vinegar, miscellaneous vegetables, and various spices. Through the eighteenth and nineteenth centuries, homemakers and chefs in Britain and North America cooked up all sorts of ketchup variations, including mushroom ketchup, walnut ketch-up, and oyster ketchup.

In the early nineteenth century, thanks to the rising popularity of the tomato in North America (it was originally a South American and Central American crop), homemade tomato ketchup became a big hit. Beginning in the 1830s, bottled tomato ketchup took off. It eventually edged out other ketchup varieties, mainly because it was so cheap to produce. Early bottled tomato ketchup was essentially a by-product of tomato canning; canneries collected juice and irregular or rotten tomato pieces that were left over from the canning process and dumped them into barrels to ferment. They boiled the fermented muck, skimmed off the scum at the top, and combined the rest with vinegar and spices to make ketchup.

Some manufacturers called their products catsup, and others called them ketchup. Both words continue to live on, causing much ado about nothing in the condiment aisles of grocery stores.

Q Why do men like to barbeque?

A Think about it: Have you ever been to a barbeque where the lady of the house flipped the burgers and brats on the grill outside with a beer in hand? It's just a fact of life that when the barbeque's fired up, there's a man hunkered over it doing the cooking—even if the slob refuses even to make a can of soup in the kitchen under normal circumstances.

And yet the leading minds of our country can give no definitive explanation of the phenomenon. Even a scholarly book called *Why Do Men Barbeque?*—published by the Harvard University Press, no less—avoids the subject, despite the title. Nary a mention of why men do the barbequing. But we're pretty sure we know why, and the answer stems from two deep-rooted anthropological realities: (1) Men have traditionally done the hunting in the human clan, and (2) men have traditionally done the religious sacrifices. And barbequing evokes features of both.

First, the hunting. In the days before McDonald's and Arby's, men left the clan and went in search of food, ideally something huge and meaty. If they succeeded in bagging the beast, they might have roasted some of it on the spot to ensure that they had the energy to drag the rest of the carcass back home. And once the men got it home, they would probably still be in charge of the cooking—roasting an elk or a mammoth had to be a big, messy, hot, and fiery affair, requiring masculine strength and physical courage. Furthermore, when there was a beast being roasted, other hungry, cranky humanoids noticed it for miles, so it was best that the male hunters were there protecting the barbeque.

That's part of our educated guess. The other part has to do with sacrifice. Ancient literature is full of evocative scenes of men—it's always men—roasting meat on open fires. The first few wisps of smoke from the meat—which we still recognize with longing, even in our suburban backyards—were considered to be especially sacred, an offering to the gods for the meal that was about to be consumed. Once you see a barbeque as a reenactment of this prehistoric spiritual drama, it's easy to imagine how the decidedly un-politically correct gender roles of the ancient world would be replicated in our own backyards, for better or worse.

In general, barbequing is a different affair from cooking indoors. It harks back to the day of hunters facing dangers and making offerings to their gods, all while guarding their hard-won quarry. The women? They were indoors grinding meal for bread—no less important, but presumably safer.

But the times, they are a-changin'. So any woman reader who wants to strike a blow for a new millennium of gender enlightenment is encouraged to send her man back into the house to prepare the couscous salad and braised asparagus while she takes up the spatula and tongs, cold beer in hand.

Q Why don't they make mouse-flavored cat food?

A There's no denying that cats have a thing for mice. It begins with the thrill of the chase, and if all goes as planned (for the cat), it ends with the satisfaction of downing a wiggling bundle of fur and bones, squeak and all.

It's feline instinct, but it's not entirely unlike the way you hit the couch, reach for the remote control, turn on the television, enjoy the thrill of a cop-show chase, and stuff your face with those special potato chips—the cheap, greasy ones that you'd never admit to loving. What's the similarity? For both the cat and for you, it's the easiest thing that's available because it's right in front of you. It's low-hanging fruit, so to speak.

If a mouse is so brazen or so foolish as to wander into Tabby's territory, the cat is going to make entertainment and a snack out of it. If that television is just going to sit there and if those chips are simply going to take up cupboard space, your best option is to make entertainment and a snack out of them. Get the idea?

A cat would rather dine on, say, a tuna, but there aren't any flopping around your family rec room. Felines don't prefer to eat mice; they eat them because they're convenient prey. Remember, cats also dine on bugs—and you don't see bug-flavored cat food at your local pet store, do you?

Q How can you identify a poisonous mushroom?

A Every gourmet knows that mushrooms can be among nature's delicacies—grilled portobello, stir-fried shiitake, and sauteed chanterelle mushrooms are mouth-watering treats. But what about the Destroying Angel, Weeping Fairy Cake, and Death Cap? As you can deduce from their names, these fungi don't belong anywhere near your lips.

How can you tell the good guys from the bad guys? There's no foolproof method—in fact, some of the most dangerous varieties are nearly indistinguishable from their edible cousins. The poisonous jack-o'-lantern mushroom, with its brightly colored cap, is easily mistaken for a yellow chanterelle. The delicious curly morel, characterized by a "brain-shaped" whorl, has an evil twin in the false morel, which also sports a spiraled top. One of the most deadly mushrooms, the brown-capped *Galerina,* looks as innocent as the varieties you'll find on your grocer's shelves.

Contrary to folk wisdom, boiling poisonous mushrooms will not neutralize their toxins. And don't assume that a fungus is safe just because you see a squirrel taking a nibble; animals can sometimes digest substances that would be fatal to human beings. Then what signs can you rely on? Naturalists suggest that you avoid any red-topped mushrooms with white dots. They may look like the cute toadstools in children's storybooks, but the *fly agaric* contains a powerful hallucinogenic substance, *muscimol,* that can send you on a really bad trip. If you see a ring high on a mushroom's stem and a cup where the stem meets the ground, chances are you've found an *Amanita phalloides*—the infamous Death Cap.

The umbrella-shaped green-spored *Lepiota* also has a ring around its stem. *Lepiota* often cluster in "fairy rings" in meadows or on lawns. Though they're not lethal, they can give you a serious case of gastric distress. Above all, keep away from LBMs, or Little Brown Mushrooms. Ranging in color from pale tan to dark chestnut, most are harmless, but you never know if a deadly *Galerina* lurks among them.

If you want to go mushroom hunting, invest in a field guide, such as those published by the Audubon society. Remember, however, that mushrooms in the wild are rarely picture-perfect—age and the damage caused by weather, insects, and animals can alter a mushroom's appearance and eradicate many of the telltale signs of danger.

The best advice is to never eat a mushroom that seems the least bit suspect. If you exercise an extra measure of caution and common sense, you'll find that you can have your favorite fungi and eat them, too.

Q Why is there a worm in some bottles of tequila?

A There are a lot of misconceptions regarding the tequila worm. First, it's not actually tequila that comes with a worm; second, the worm isn't really a worm; and finally, the whole worm-in-a-bottle thing isn't part of any Mexican tradition.

Tequila is a specific form of mezcal, a Mexican liquor made by distilling juices from the agave plant. Mezcal can be made from any of the more than four hundred species of the agave plant; tequila must contain at least 51 percent blue agave. (High-quality tequila uses 100 percent blue agave.) Tequila is closely regulated by the Mexican government and comes only from certain parts of southwestern Mexico. Other mezcal liquors originate from all over the country, and they vary widely both in quality and composition.

You will not find a worm in a bottle of true tequila, but you might run across one in a bottle of mezcal. The worms are larvae from various insect species that feed off agave plants, so they're actually caterpillars or grubs.

There are pervasive legends about the so-called worm. For example, the presence of a worm is said to demonstrate that the mezcal is a high proof, and eating it is supposed to supercharge your sex drive and cause hallucinations. In truth, the worm originated as a marketing gimmick, hatched by mezcal bottler Jacobo Lozano Paez around 1950. As the story goes, Paez noticed that larvae on agave plants sometimes got mixed up in the juices used to make mezcal, and he thought that they added a distinctive taste. To set his mezcal apart, Paez dropped a larva into each bottle. The gimmick made mezcal seem more exotic to Americans, and the legend was born.

The larvae are not psychedelic, and there's not much evidence that they are aphrodisiacs. But if you want to eat them anyway, knock yourself out. Legitimate mezcal makers that include a worm in the bottle typically raise larvae explicitly for this purpose, so they are likely to be pesticide-free. Besides, if you make it to the bottom of a mezcal bottle, larva contaminants will be the least of your health concerns.

Q Who invented food-on-a-stick?

A Corn dogs, popsicles, cotton candy, and candy apples—some of America's best treats are served up on a stick. Really, what's more fun than kabobbing around a summer carnival with a stick of corn in one hand and cheesecake-on-a-stick in the other?

How about adding fried pickles, sloppy joes, alligator sausage, or spaghetti and meatballs to your food-on-a-stick shtick? At the Minnesota State Fair, held annually over Labor Day weekend, you'll find some sixty-nine different foodstuffs that are offered up on a stick, ranging from the traditional to the completely outlandish. Corned beef and cabbage on a stick? You got it. Don't forget to wash it all down with an espresso-on-a-stick—frozen espresso, of course.

Yep, those Minnesota State Fair vendors have taken the food-on-a-stick concept to a whole new level of culinary genius. But the truth is, people have been using sticks, skewers, poles, and spits to cook and serve up food for centuries. That's why it's so confoundingly difficult to say who came up with the idea in the first place.

Most people agree that the original food-on-a-stick was probably the shish kebab. But who invented the kebab? Some say that it was the nomadic Turkish soldiers who invaded and conquered Anatolia—the heartland of modern-day Turkey—in the eleventh century. According to legend, these warriors used swords to grill their meat over their campfires as they moved westward from Central Asia.

But don't tell that to the Greeks—or to Mediterranean food expert Clifford A. Wright. According to this James Beard Foundation Award winner, there's plenty of iconographical evidence to suggest that the ancient Greeks were skewering up shish kebabs as early as the eighth century BC, well before the Turks blazed their destructive (yet tasty) trail into the region. Want proof? Just dig up your copy of Homer's *The Odyssey.*

We may never know the true inventor of the concept, but one thing's for sure: Food-on-a-stick is popular in almost every culture in the world. The Japanese have their yakitori, the French have their brochettes, and we have our Pronto Pups.

But who exactly invented that quintessentially American cornbread-coated wiener-on-a-stick? As you might expect, this question is hotly debated. Claimants to the title include Jack Karnis, the Fletcher brothers (Carl and Neil), and the Cozy Dog Drive In of Springfield, Illinois.

Who knew food-on-a-stick could be such a sticky subject?

Q Why do we tip some service people but not others?

A The practical reason is that tipping is built into the pay structure for certain jobs. In the United States, employers set wages for certain jobs with the expectation that tips will be a big part of an employee's income. These jobs include restaurant food servers, food-delivery drivers, bartenders, hair stylists, hotel housekeepers, bellhops, taxi drivers, and valets. In many cases, base pay for these jobs is less than minimum wage, and gratuities make up the difference.

You may see tip jars at, say, coffee shops, but Americans don't feel societal pressure to tip on every visit to these establishments. Nor do the livelihoods of the baristas depend on tips. In full-service restaurants, on the other hand, most people know that you should tip a server 15 to 20 percent and that the server depends on this money.

Where did these rules come from? For many "tipping professions," the tradition dates back to the English aristocracy in the seventeenth and eighteenth centuries. When the well-to-do visited each other's estates for extended periods, they typically rewarded the host's servants with "vails"—something extra at the end of stays as thanks for tending to the rooms and other needs. (It would have been simply dreadful not to pay the help. What would it have said about one's own assets?) This type of peer pressure eventually forced vails into common practice at commercial establishments.

The practice took hold among the well-to-do in the United States following the Civil War. Though many people publicly condemned the practice as anti-American because it seemed to propagate the notion of rigidly separated classes, tipping gradually spread beyond homes to the equivalents of domestic servers, maids, valets, and others at inns and restaurants. Americans also began to tip for some additional services (i.e., shoe shining, coat checks, taxis).

Today, tipping traditions are associated with the type of service and not with the wealth of the customer. Eating at the Waffle

House may be a far cry from fine dining among the English aristocracy, but Waffle House servers are still part of a tradition that began on seventeenth-century estates. Fast-food workers, on the other hand, don't tend to your needs during a meal, so they fall in the tradition of street vendors, in which tipping never took root. Of course, if you buck the trend and tip them anyway, you might get an extra ketchup packet out of the deal.

Q Did Alice B. Toklas invent the hash brownie?

A Alice B. Toklas is famous for two reasons: First, people often assume that she was the author and subject of the 1933 book *The Autobiography of Alice B. Toklas;* second, she's often credited with concocting the recipe for brownies that is loaded with hashish, the psychotropic resin extracted from the flowering top of a cannabis plant.

But the truth is, Alice didn't do either of these things. No, the poet and author Gertrude Stein penned *The Autobiography of Alice B. Toklas,* framing it as the personal memoir of Toklas, who was her longtime lover. The book is more an autobiography of Stein than of Toklas—it delves into Stein's famous friendships with Pablo Picasso, Henri Matisse, and Ernest Hemingway, among other topics.

After Stein died, Toklas published her own memoir of sorts, *The Alice B. Toklas Cookbook,* a mix of autobiography and recipes. The 1954 book includes a recipe for "Haschich Fudge," but Toklas didn't come up with it. Toklas didn't have enough of her own recipes to fill the book, so she asked friends to help out. As a joke, an artist friend named Brion Gysin submitted a recipe for a brownie-like dessert that was loaded with marijuana. The recipe recommended the dessert as a treat for a ladies bridge club, promising "euphoria and brilliant storms of laughter; ecstatic reveries and extensions of one's personality on several simultaneous planes."

The scandalous ingredient—listed as "canibus [sic] sativa"—sailed right past Toklas, who was in her seventies at the time and was hardly a drug connoisseur. However, the editors at Harper's caught it and cut the recipe from the American edition. British publishers, though, kept it in their edition, and the media made a big deal of the trippy recipe.

Jokes about Toklas's special brownie recipe took root, fueled by the 1968 Peter Sellers movie *I Love You, Alice B. Toklas.* (The movie doesn't have anything to do with Toklas—Sellers plays a straight-laced man who drops out of society to become a hippie after eating the Toklas brownies.)

The book popularized hashish brownies, although it's not clear whether Gysin came up with the recipe himself. At the time, he co-owned a restaurant in Tangier, Morocco, where marijuana-loaded food was popular. So it simply may have been a local recipe.

Besides, marijuana treats were nothing new when the book was published. More than three thousand years ago, people in India and China were eating hashish and mixing it with food. You can hardly hold Alice B. Toklas responsible for those bold and exciting culinary experiments.

Q How do they make pink wine if there are no pink grapes?

A Here at F.Y.I. headquarters, we're dedicated to bringing you the most accurate answers to life's important questions. So we spent a lot of time and sacrificed many liver cells at a local vineyard researching this one.

During one particularly lengthy and arduous tasting session, we peppered the vintner with questions about wine production. He answered many of our queries quite pleasantly. The wine flowed. We became brazen. Finally, we asked him to show us his pink grapes. Embarrassment ensued.

It turns out that there are no pink grapes. Pink wines—known to oenophiles as roses—are made from red grapes. Understanding why requires a short lesson in general wine-making.

Grapes are put into a crusher, where their juice is extracted and stems and skins are separated from the grape flesh. The flesh and juice of all grapes is basically colorless—wine made from just these elements will be white, regardless of the color of grape skin. This explains why pinot grigio grapes, which can be very dark in color, produce a white wine.

If green grapes are used, the skins are usually removed because green grape skins add little to a white wine. The skins of red grapes, however, bring benefits that include tannins—the element that provides the mouth-puckering feel of dry wines—and an antioxidant called resveratrol. Perhaps most important, including the skins of red and purple grapes in the fermentation process imparts color to the finished product. The amount of contact that is allowed between the grape juice and the grape skins largely determines the color of the wine.

Which brings us back to the pressing question at hand: pink wines. Take white zinfandel (which actually is pink). The zinfandel grape is red. During production, vintners who wish to produce a white zinfandel permit the skins of the grapes to have partial contact with the wine. This tints the wine but doesn't allow it to reach the full red color. Our vintner said that pink wines can also be made by mixing a little red wine with white, although this is rarely done.

And so our inquiry came to a conclusion without revealing any pink grapes. We did, however, eventually see more than a few pink elephants.

Chapter Eight

EARTH AND SPACE

Q How do we know that no two snowflakes are alike?

A Well, do you know the Snowflake Man? In 1885, Wilson A. Bentley became the first person to photograph a single snow crystal. By cleverly adapting a microscope to a bellows camera, the nineteen-year-old perfected a process that allowed him to catch snowflakes on a black-painted wooden tray and then capture their images before they melted away.

A self-educated farmer from the rural town of Jericho, Vermont, Bentley would go on to attract worldwide attention for his pioneering work in the field of photomicrography. In 1920, the American Meteorological Society elected him as a fellow and later awarded him its very first research grant, a whopping twenty-five dollars.

Over forty-seven years, Bentley captured 5,381 pictographs of individual snowflakes. Near the end of his life, the Snowflake Man said that he had never seen two snowflakes that were alike: "Under the microscope, I found that snowflakes were miracles of beauty. Every crystal was a masterpiece of design and no one design was ever repeated."

Since Bentley's original observation, physicists, snowologists, crystallographers, and meteorologists have continued to photograph and study the different patterns of ice-crystal growth and snowflake formation (with more technologically advanced equipment, of course). But guess what? Bentley's snow story sticks.

Even today, scientists agree: It is extremely unlikely that two snowflakes can be exactly alike. It's so unlikely, in fact, that Kenneth G. Libbrecht, a professor of physics at Caltech, says, "Even if you looked at every one ever made, you would not find any exact duplicates."

How so? Says Libbrecht, "The number of possible ways of making a complex snowflake is staggeringly large." A snowflake may start out as a speck of dust, but as it falls through the clouds, it gathers up more than 180 billion water molecules. These water molecules freeze, evaporate, and arrange themselves into endlessly inventive patterns under the influence of endless environmental conditions.

And that's just it—snow crystals are so sensitive to the tiniest fluctuations in temperature and atmosphere that they're constantly changing in shape and structure as they gently fall to the ground. Molecule for molecule, it's virtually impossible for two snow crystals to have the exact same pattern of development and design.

"It is probably safe to say that the possible number of snow crystal shapes exceeds the estimated number of atoms in the known universe," says Jon Nelson, a cloud physicist who has studied snowflakes for fifteen years. Still, we can't be 100 percent sure that no two snowflakes are exactly alike—we're just going to have to take science's word for it. Each winter, trillions upon trillions of snow crystals drop from the sky. Are *you* going to check them all out?

Q What is the speed of dark?

A Most of us believe that nothing is faster than the speed of light. In high school physics, we learned that something traveling faster than light speed could theoretically go back in time. This would allow for the possibility that you could go back in time and kill your grandfather and, thus, negate your existence—a scenario known as the Grandfather Paradox. Or more horrifyingly, you could go back in time in order to set up your future parents as you skateboard around to the musical stylings of Huey Lewis and the News.

Yet there is something that may be faster than the speed of light: the speed of dark. Or maybe not. The speed of dark may not even exist. When you're talking about astrophysics and quantum mechanics, nothing is certain (indeed, uncertainty might be said to be the defining principle of modern physics).

Observations and experiments in recent years have helped astrophysicists shape a more comprehensive understanding of how the universe operates, but even the most brilliant scientists are operating largely on guesswork. To understand how the speed of dark theoretically might—or might not—exceed the speed of light, we'll have to get into some concepts that are usually reserved for late-night bong sessions.

As with much of astronomy, our explanation is rooted in the Big Bang. For those of you who slept through science class or were raised in the Bible Belt, the Big Bang is the prevailing scientific explanation for the creation of the universe. According to the Big Bang theory, the universe started as a pinpoint of dense, hot matter. About fourteen billion years ago, this infinitely dense point exploded, sending the foundations of the universe into the outer reaches of space.

The momentum from this initial explosion caused the universe to expand as it drove the boundaries outward. For most of the twentieth century, the prevailing thought was that the rate of expansion was slowing down and would eventually grind to a halt. Seemed logical enough, right?

In 1998, however, astronomers participating in two top-secret-sounding research projects, the Supernova Cosmology Project and the High-Z Supernova Search, made a surprising discovery while observing supernovae events (exploding stars) in the distant reaches of space. Supernovae are handy for astronomers because just prior to exploding, these stars reach a uniform brightness.

Why is this important? The stars provide a standard variable, allowing scientists to infer other statistics, such as how far the stars are from Earth. Once scientists know a star's distance from Earth, they can use another phenomenon known as a redshift (a visual analogue to the Doppler effect in which light appears differently to the observer because an object is moving away from him or her) to determine how much the universe has expanded since the explosion.

Still with us? Now, based on what scientists had previously believed, supernovae should have appeared brighter than what the redshift indicated. But to the scientists' amazement, the supernovae appeared dimmer, indicating that the expansion of the universe is speeding up, not slowing down. How could this be? And if the expansion is quickening, what is it that's driving it forward and filling up that empty space?

Initially nobody had any real idea. But after much discussion, theorists came up with the idea of dark energy. What is dark energy? Ultimately, it's a made-up term for the inexplicable and incomprehensible emptiness of deep space. For the purposes of our question, however, one important attribute is that dark energy is far faster than the speed of light—it's so fast, in fact, that it is moving too quickly for new stars to form in the empty space. No, it doesn't make a whole heck of a lot of sense to us either, but rest assured, a lot of very nerdy people have spent a long time studying it.

Of course, there may be a far simpler answer, one posited by science-fiction writer Terry Pratchett: The speed of dark *must* be faster than the speed of light—otherwise, how would dark be able to get out of the way?

Q Does running through the rain keep you drier than walking?

A It makes intuitive sense that running through the rain will keep you drier than walking. You will spend less time in the rain, after all. But there's a pervasive old wives' tale that says it won't do any good. So every time there's a downpour and you need to get to your car, you are faced with this confounding question: Should you walk or run?

The argument against running is that more drops hit your chest and legs when you're moving at a quicker pace. If you're walking, the theory goes, the drops are mainly hitting your head. So the proponents of walking say that running exposes you to more drops, not fewer.

Several scientists have pondered this possibility (after finishing up their actual work for the day, we hope). In 1987, an Italian physicist determined that sprinting keeps you drier than walking, but only by about 10 percent, which might not be worth the effort and the risk of slipping. In 1995, a British researcher concluded that the increased front-drenching of running effectively cancels out the reduced rain exposure.

These findings didn't seem right to two climatologists at the National Climatic Data Center in Asheville, North Carolina, so they decided to put them to the test. In 1996, they put on identical outfits with plastic bags underneath to keep moisture from seeping out of the clothes and to keep their own sweat from adding to the drenching. One person ran about 330 feet in the rain; the other walked the same distance. They weighed the wet clothes, compared the weights to those when the clothes were dry, and determined that the climatologist who walked got 40 percent wetter than the one who ran.

In other words, run to your car. You're justified—no matter how silly you might look.

Q Are there flesh-eating plants?

A Once upon a time, a hapless florist named Seymour Krelborn discovered a strange plant in his shop that had a taste for blood. If you're a fan of off-Broadway musicals, you'll recognize this as the plot of *Little Shop of Horrors*.

Seymour's potted pal might have been a fantasy, but flesh-eating plants do exist. The most famous is the Venus flytrap, whose pair of spiky, hinged petals snap shut on unsuspecting insects. Though the Venus flytrap might sound exotic, it's actually an all-American species that's found in the bogs and swamps of Florida, the Carolinas, and occasionally as far north as New Jersey.

Another well-known botanical carnivore is the pitcher plant. As its name implies, the plant's blossom is shaped like a narrow pitcher and filled with a deadly nectar that lures insects inside. Pitcher plants come in many varieties and are found in Europe, South America, and North America. One type, native to northern California and Oregon, has been dubbed the cobra plant, a sinister reference to its long, curved snake-like flower and mottled coloring.

The third-most common type of carnivorous plant is the so-called "flypaper" trap. The butterwort—found in Europe, North America, South America, Central America, and south Asia—is a good example of this variety. The thick, "buttery" leaves of this non-descript ground plant are coated with insect-trapping mucus.

Technically, all of these plants are insectivores, not carnivores. (*Carne* comes from the Latin word for "flesh.") So do any plants literally consume flesh? Large pitcher plants in South America have been known to digest frogs, small birds, and even tiny rodents, although this isn't their usual fare. People who cultivate carnivorous plants sometimes feed them bits of meat. But experts at the International Carnivorous Plant Society (ICPS) caution against this practice, pointing out that the enzymes these plants use to absorb nutrients are better adapted to insects and that the plants are likely to starve on a steady diet of beef and chicken.

Barry Rice, author of *Growing Carnivorous Plants,* confesses to feeding a few Venus flytraps fragments of skin that were sloughed from his own toes during a bout with athlete's foot. Much to his surprise, the traps took to these unappetizing tidbits. Unlike Audrey in *Little Shop of Horrors,* however, Rice's plants did not begin crooning, "Feed me! Feed me!" Be assured that any reports you hear of plants that are big enough to consume a human be-ing are strictly figments of Hollywood's imagination.

In fact, carnivorous plants face a far greater threat from humans than vice versa. Development has threatened the habitats of many plants. Of the approximately 630 species of carnivorous plants identified by biologists, the ICPS estimates that twenty-six are currently imperiled. Carnivorous plants help balance the ecosystem by keeping insect populations in check. Without them, the planet might become a shop of horrors, indeed.

Q How do we know what's in Earth's core?

A The moles aren't talking, so we've had to figure it out the hard way. Geologists say that the center of Earth is a massive metal core. The inner section of the core, which is about 1,500 miles in diameter, is mostly iron and contains some nickel. Surrounding the inner section is a 1,400-mile-thick layer of liquid iron and nickel called the outer core. This core is covered by an extremely hot, slow-moving liquid called the mantle that is 1,800 miles thick; the mantle accounts for the bulk of the planet's mass. Above the mantle is the outer crust, five to thirty miles thick and made up of cool rock, on top of which is where we live and play.

We are familiar with the crust, and we sometimes see evidence of the mantle from volcanic eruptions. Everything we know about the areas below the mantle comes from guesswork and clever remote measurements.

The most useful measurement device is the earthquake. Vibrations from an earthquake generate seismic waves that not only move across the surface of the crust, but also through the planet's interior. Just like light waves, seismic waves change speeds as they pass through different types of material. One effect of changing speeds is that the waves refract (turn) at the boundaries between two layers, just as light refracts at the boundary between air and water or as it goes through a lens. Earthquakes produce two types of waves—P waves and S waves—that move through material distinctly and provide seismologists with lots of data.

By noting the time it takes for waves to travel through the planet and observing the patterns of these waves, seismologists have estimated the general densities and locations of different layers of material. The most striking piece of data is a massive "shadow zone" of S waves. Essentially, something in Earth's core blocks S waves that are generated on one side of the planet from reaching the opposite side of the planet.

This suggests that part of Earth's core is liquid, since S waves can move through solid material but not liquid. P waves can move through liquid; their patterns indicate that they encounter an inner solid core after the liquid layer. The intense pressure at the center of the planet apparently prevents the inner core from liquefying.

There's one final piece of the puzzle. All of the planets came from the same swirling mass of matter that formed the solar system. Based on the composition of meteorites left over from this original space junk, scientists have determined the general mix of elements that would have gone into forming Earth. This analysis shows that the planet should include a huge amount of iron, which isn't accounted for in Earth's crust, atmosphere, or mantle. So it must be in the core. As a young Earth was cooling, the heavy iron presumably sank to the center. If only the moles could tell us for certain.

Q Does sound travel quicker through water or air?

A When you came across this question in the table of contents, you probably thought, "Everyone knows the answer to that one. It's *so* obvious." This, of course, is exactly why we chose to include it. Once again, it is our honored duty to inform you that you are 100 percent wrong. Sound actually travels much faster through water than air. We'll get to the hows and whys in a moment, but let's start with the reason that you and everyone who is not an engineer were so sure that you knew the correct answer.

The confusion probably stems from the fact that we humans are designed to process sound waves that are transmitted through air, not water. Perhaps you learned this as a child at the local swimming pool, when you and your buddy dipped your heads beneath the surface and then attempted to communicate. Although you may have heard *something*, it was most likely an unintelligible gurgle.

The act of turning vibrations into sounds involves a series of bones in the inner ear—the malleus, incus, and stapes—and bone conductivity is 40 percent less effective underwater. Furthermore, when the auditory canal fills with water, the eardrum (another major aspect involved in the sensation of hearing) doesn't vibrate properly. As a result, many people just assume that sound travels less efficiently through water.

But the truth is, sound travels approximately five times faster through water than air. We say "approximately" because there are several variables to consider, such as temperature, altitude, and humidity. But whether you are talking about cold air or warm water, there must be some sort of medium in order to facilitate the transmission of sound waves. (There is no sound in the vacuum of space.)

Essentially, sound waves are just molecules bouncing off of other molecules until they reach your ears and are processed as sound. Because water is denser than air, these molecules are packed closer together and sound waves are able to travel at a greater velocity. For the same reason, sound can travel farther through water than air before dissipating. (Sound, in fact, travels fastest through solids such as metal. That's why people have been known to put an ear to a rail to hear if a train is approaching.)

Gases such as air are relatively poor conductors of sound—they just happen to be the right environment for the human auditory system. So, yes, we kind of set you up with this one—and for that, we apologize. It was all in the name of providing you with a nugget of valuable knowledge.

Q Where did the moon come from?

A Before Neil and Buzz had a chance to poke around up there, astronomers had three competing theories to explain the origin of the moon, based strictly on their observations of it from a great distance.

The co-accretion, or condensation, theory stated that the moon formed out of swirling space dust and gas at the same time as Earth, 4.5 billion years ago. The fission theory, meanwhile, speculated that the newly formed Earth was spinning so fast that it shed a bunch of debris that clumped together to form the moon. And the capture theory held that the moon was a wandering asteroid that meandered past Earth and got snagged by its gravitational pull.

Everyone hoped that hands-on analysis of the moon would clear things up. But the rocks that were collected by astronauts from the lunar surface didn't validate any of these explanations—on the contrary, each theory was cast into further doubt.

Moon rock turned out to be similar to Earth rock, which made the wandering asteroid idea seem unlikely. But oddly enough, moon rock is completely dry, while the minerals of Earth contain significant amounts of moisture. This discovery worked against the fission theory, since spun-off Earth debris would likely retain some water content. The fission theory was further undermined when the samples' densities suggested that the moon once had an entirely molten surface, which wouldn't have been possible if the debris had simply peeled off of Earth.

Finally, seismic readings taken by the astronauts showed that the moon is much less dense than Earth and has a much smaller inner core, if it has a core at all. This observation called the co-accretion theory into question. Why? Presumably, two planetary bodies that formed in the same spot at the same time would have more similarities in their structures than the seismic readings indicated.

The ensuing head-scratching sparked a fourth, more radical idea that is called the giant-impact, or giant-impactor, theory.

In this scenario, the moon is the result of a Mars-size rock (a leftover from the solar system's birth) that slammed into Earth about 4.45 billion years ago. This collision sent huge chunks of Earth and the impactor into orbit. Some debris flew off into outer space, some debris fell back to Earth, and over the course of time, the rest of the hot rock in orbit clumped together to form the moon.

This is the leading theory today because it best fits the evidence. First, it's consistent with the composition of moon rock: The intense heat of the impact could have vaporized any water that was in the flying debris, and it could have given the moon its once-molten surface. The theory also explains why the moon may not have a core: It was formed mainly from Earth's crust material, so it has something similar to that consistency throughout. The many giant craters on the moon also support the notion that there were a lot of giant flying rocks zipping around the solar system in the old days.

All things considered, it appears as if Earth was lucky to lose only a moon-size chunk.

Chapter Nine

HISTORY

Q Was math discovered or invented?

A This question has been kicked around by just about every serious philosopher over the past 2,500 years or so. In that light, it might seem somewhat curious to find it discussed in the same book that brings you questions like "Whom do we blame for the mullet hairstyle?" But, hey, we're not afraid to tackle the tough ones.

Invented things didn't exist before they were invented. They may meet a pressing, timeless human need—such as, you know, the electric foot-callus sander—but they weren't around until a light-bulb went off in someone's head.

Discovered things always have existed, such as the element strontium. It's been around forever, but nobody knew it until 1787 when Scottish miners near the village of Strontian found it in the mineral strontianite.

Where does math fit in? To many folks, math is simply a symbolic representation of the real, physical world. You can call the number two "two" or you can call it "Shirley," but the concept underlying 2 + 2 = 4 has always been there. When man figured out that concept, he discovered math. This is what Plato felt.

But others question this belief on fairly abstract philosophical grounds, essentially saying that if math "existed" before we conceived of it or discovered it, then we have to accept the existence of an abstract notion even without human brains there to be aware of it. Philosophers call this "theism," and apparently it makes some of them nervous.

To us—the same people, we warn you, who brought you an answer to "Are fat people more jolly?"—it makes sense that math was discovered. Math is a specific, precise, rigorous way of describing the physical world, involving hard-and-fast rules. There are different ways of expressing or arriving at the concept of "four," but that concept is always distinct from "five" in precisely the same way; you can't say that four things are five things. This reality was there as soon as there were four things in the universe, even though people weren't around to understand it.

We're getting into metaphysics here—"If a tree falls in the forest..." stuff—but that's the way philosophy is. Makes your high school geometry seem pretty straightforward in comparison, doesn't it?

Q Who's the fastest guitarist on the planet?

A A fair follow-up question is, "Who cares?" But the truth is, lots of guys really do care—even if most of them still live in their parents' basements.

You don't have to be a Freudian psychologist to guess why a dude clutching a guitar is evocative of certain primal urges, and so there is a macho cachet to being the fastest guitarist on the planet, as there is to guitar proficiency in general. If you still don't understand this, ask your girlfriend. Or ask Keith Richards, who still manages to attract hot women despite looking like something you'd find living under a bridge.

So it's cool to be fast, and guitar magazines and Web sites are full of speculation and "analysis" about who is the fastest. These guys—and with possibly one exception, they all seem to be guys—are nicknamed "shredders." (As in, "Dude, this fifteen-minute atonal guitar solo totally shreds!") If you're gonna play fast, it helps to be playing something repetitive and familiar, so a lot of these guys play "tunes" based on scales and other familiar melodic patterns.

For example, famed Swedish shredder Yngwie Malmsteen was captivated by the violin music of Niccolo Paganini as a child and has made a supposedly lucrative career out of bringing the master's melodies to his distorted Fender Stratocaster guitar. If you think that this classical inspiration sounds kind of lame, bear in mind that Yngwie is no poindexter: Supposedly, he once menaced a flight attendant who spilled water on him, screaming at her, "You have unleashed the [bleep]ing fury!"

Anyway, Yngwie tops many "fastest" lists, as does Michael Angelo Batio, a guy who looks like he stole Jeff Beck's hair, put it on steroids, and then planted it on his own head. Batio truly is fast, and he intensifies the effect by playing a "double guitar" that has two separate necks. Basically, his fingers tap the strings as if they were tiny piano keys, so both hands are playing furiously at the same time. Reportedly, he also owns a "quad guitar"—speculate all you want as to which appendages handle the extra shredding duties.

Another top candidate for fastest of the fast is The Great Kat—one of the only women to find success in this testosterone-fueled scene. She's a truly preposterous classically trained musician who has taken to transcribing the canon to guitar, donning "sexy" S&M clothing and doing her shredding while making grotesque faces. Some dudes are in love with her—there's simply no accounting for taste.

And then there's Tiago Della Vega, a young Brazilian who really might be the fastest on the planet. By some estimates, he plays 320 beats per minute. Don't expect to find a real melody in there. If you don't get tired of him after about thirty seconds, you're a fan of shred.

Chances are, you're probably also still living in your parents' basement.

Q Why do we call someone a dark-horse candidate?

A In 1831, Benjamin Disraeli (who became the British prime minister thirty-seven years later) used the term "dark horse" in a novel to describe an unknown horse that won a race and surprised everyone. After that, a dark horse could mean any contestant in sports or politics who didn't look promising but who might unexpectedly win.

In the 1844 U.S. presidential race, the expected nominee for the Democrats was Martin Van Buren. Van Buren argued against the annexation of Texas, though, which cost him the support of many delegates at the Democratic convention. There were no super delegates in those days, so the convention went through eight rounds of voting before the delegates selected a compromise candidate: James K. Polk, who had not even appeared on the first seven ballots. Months later, Polk was elected president. Since he literally came out of nowhere to win the ultimate prize, he is considered to be the first dark-horse candidate for president.

There have been others: James Garfield garnered the Republican nomination on the thirty-sixth ballot and won the general election by a scant ten thousand votes. When he was assassinated just months after taking office, his vice president, Chester Arthur, became president, which made him a sort of dark horse, too.

Not impressed? In 1860, an obscure Illinois lawyer came out of the woodwork to capture the nomination of the upstart Republican Party. Since the Democrats had split into factions, and the only other serious party, the Whigs, had collapsed, Abraham Lincoln became president. To many, he was the ultimate dark horse.

Q What's the point of the electoral college?

A You've heard the mantra as each presidential election approaches: "Get out and vote! Every vote counts!" Well, guess what? That's not exactly true. Under the electoral college system, we don't elect the president through a direct, nationwide popular vote. The electoral college decides the outcome.

Just ask Al Gore. In the 2000 election, he beat George W. Bush in the nationwide popular ballot by more than five hundred thousand votes. However, in the electoral college, Gore was outdone by Bush, 271 to 266. And Bush was the new president.

This wasn't the only time a candidate who carried the popular vote didn't win a trip to the Oval Office. In 1888, Grover Cleveland got 90,596 more votes than Benjamin Harrison, but Harrison won the electoral college by sixty-five votes. In 1876, Samuel J. Tilden got 254,235 more votes than Rutherford B. Hayes, but Hayes prevailed in the electoral college—by one vote!

Are you wondering just who came up with this cockamamie system? The electoral voting process was designed by the framers of the U.S. Constitution (you know, our founding fathers). These political leaders believed that it was unfair to give Congress the sole power to select the president, but they also feared that a purely popular election would be reckless. (Ordinary citizens weren't considered to be informed enough to choose wisely.) And so they came up with the electoral voting system as a compromise.

Proponents of the electoral college system say that it works because a candidate must garner wide geographic support to win the presidency. They point out that it also protects the interests of smaller states that might otherwise be ignored if not for the power of their electoral votes. (Consider that if Gore had won tiny New Hampshire in 2000, the electoral vote would have swayed in his favor and he would have been president.)

Opponents of the electoral college argue that it's wholly undemocratic that the winner of the popular vote can lose the election. They also claim that there isn't an incentive for voters to turn out in states where one party is clearly dominant, and that the system penalizes third-party candidates. (In 1992, Ross Perot won a whopping 19 percent of the national popular vote, but he garnered no electoral votes.)

Is the electoral college fair? For the answer, we turn to the great Alexander Hamilton, an original proponent of the system, who said that the electoral college may not be perfect, but it's "at least excellent."

Q Who came up with the yoyo?

A The yoyo, that favorite toy among children seemingly everywhere, has both a long string and a long history. Ancient China may be the source of the first yoyo-like devices. Consisting of two porcelain disks that were connected by a metal ring, this precursor to the yoyo wasn't attached to a string but was tossed, juggled, and rolled along a taut cord, which the user held between two fingers or two sticks. Today, the technique is known in yoyo competitions as "off string."

No one knows if the Greeks were the first to attach a yoyo to a string, but a Greek vase, circa 500 BC, shows a young man playing with an object on a string that is indisputably a yoyo. Yoyos probably reached Europe via trade routes during the Middle Ages; at that time, they were called bandalores. The origin of this name is murky, but bandalores were keeping some very famous fingers busy centuries later. A French drawing from the 1780s shows the revolutionary general Marquis de Lafayette playing with one, and Napoleon was rumored to have kept his bandalore handy.

The first Americans to capitalize on the popular toy were a pair of Ohio inventors, James L. Haven and Charles Hettrich. They obtained a patent on a new, improved version of the bandalore in 1866, but the yoyo as we know it today didn't appear until 1928. That's when Filipino American Pedro Flores established the Yoyo Manufacturing Company in Santa Barbara, California.

"Yoyo," Flores told people, meant "come-come" in his native language, Tagalog. Some sources claim that Filipino tribes used yoyos for centuries to hunt small game. So unlike Westerners, they used them for work, not play.

Flores's yoyos were carved from a single piece of wood with a string that was looped, not tied, around the center axle. This innovation allowed Flores to perform many of the yoyo tricks, such as "sleeping" and "walking the dog," that continue to enthrall kids today.

Around 1930, Flores sold his company to a fellow yoyo enthusiast for a little more than $250,000, a phenomenal sum at the time. The buyer was Donald Duncan, and far as he was concerned, it was worth every penny. Duncan retained Flores as a spokesman; together, they kept yoyos spinning though the Great Depression by hosting contests and other kid-friendly promotions. By 1946, Duncan's factory was churning out 3,600 yoyos per hour. Yoyomania peaked around 1962, when the company was selling forty-five million annually, about 1.125 yoyos for every child in America.

The evolution of the yoyo continues, and thanks to lightweight materials and sophisticated engineering, a whole new repertoire of dazzling tricks is possible. Not bad for a simple toy that's been a friend to kids for millennia.

Q Why is the U.S. presidential election held on a Tuesday in November?

A Blame it on Congress. Before 1845, the U.S. presidential election was held during the first week of December. But that year, Congress designated November as the election month for both the president and members of Congress because November's weather is typically milder than December's. This, Congress felt, would ensure a better turnout since most Americans lived in rural areas back then and had to travel long distances by foot or on horseback to reach voting sites.

Why Tuesday? Some men (only white men could vote, remember) had to leave home a day in advance. A Monday election meant leaving home on Sunday, the day of worship. Friday and the weekend were not considered good options, either—as is the case today, weekends were booked with travel, shopping, and other business. And Thursday? That was Britain's election day, and the United States didn't want its political process to resemble Britain's in any way. Tuesday and Wednesday were the only other possibilities, and Tuesday was chosen.

Does it matter which Tuesday in November? Yes. It's always the Tuesday after the first Monday in November, which means elections will never be held on the first day of the month. Why is this important? At the time that the decision was made, small businesses typically closed out their October books and balanced their ledgers on the first day of November. Furthermore, November 1 is a Catholic holiday (All Saints' Day), which might have kept some men away from the voting booths.

The first election following the enactment of these rules took place on November 4, 1845. It wasn't a presidential contest—members of Congress were elected—but it nonetheless marked the beginning of an American tradition.

Q What's so great about Citizen Kane?

A Every year since 1962, *Sight & Sound* magazine's poll of film critics has ranked *Citizen Kane* as the greatest movie of all time; many directors cite it as one of their chief influences and inspirations; and the American Film Institute put it at the top of its "100 Years, 100 Movies" list. Pretty impressive for a 1941 drama about a newspaper mogul that doesn't feature a single car chase, robot battle, or panty raid. What's the big deal, anyway?

Fans of *Citizen Kane* can give you dozens of reasons why they love it, citing everything from the screenplay to the sound design to the cinematography. And that's precisely why the movie is impressive: Orson Welles pulled out every innovative storytelling technique he could come up with to spin his yarn in an original, engaging way. It comes down to style—the movie is filled with creative filmmaking tricks.

Looking at the movie as a whole, what really sticks out is the unconventional way that the plot moves through time. The film begins with the death of the main character, Kane, and then cuts to an obituary newsreel that summarizes his rise and fall. The newsreel producer wants to know the meaning of Kane's final word, "rosebud," and sends a reporter out to investigate. As the reporter talks to everyone in Kane's life, the story unfolds through flashbacks, showing Kane at many ages and from many perspectives. In the first few minutes, you learn the basic story of Kane's life, but the true meaning comes out only as you double back and look closer through the multilayered memories of his friends and enemies. This was revolutionary in 1941. Fifty years before *Pulp Fiction,* Welles and the screenwriter Herman Mankiewicz jumbled up time and asked the audience to put it back together again.

When you examine the movie closely, you can see that just about every shot was meticulously crafted. Cinematographer Gregg Toland developed deep-focus techniques in order to create busy shots in which everything is in sharp focus, from objects right in front of the camera to people far in the background. Combined with extreme low- and high-angle shots, elaborate pans, symbolic imagery, creative sound editing, and rapid cuts through time, you end up with plenty to dissect.

The film received good reviews when it was released, but it was a bomb at the box office. In the 1950s, avant-garde European filmmakers rediscovered it and built on many of its ideas. By the 1960s, it was a standard subject in U.S. film schools, largely because it includes excellent examples of many filmmaking techniques. As a result, it left a mark on the generation of cutting-edge filmmakers that made the most important movies of the 1970s and 1980s.

But if you hate *Citizen Kane,* don't feel badly—several respected film critics do, too. Guess they like more panty raids in their art films.

Q Why are Democrats on the left and Republicans on the right?

A In this era of cable-channel charlatans, jingoist radio shows, and boorish bloggers, it's tempting to see things in black and white. In political discourse, this polarization finds expression in the terms "left" and "right." Regardless of what their respective defenders and detractors might like to believe, "right" in this sense isn't a synonym for "correct." And "left" doesn't conjure up the bogeyman—even if our word "sinister" does come from *sinestra si,* Latin for "left."

The concept of the political "left" and "right" can be traced across the Atlantic Ocean to France. It came to the fore in 1789 during the French Revolution, when the National Assembly first convened. The Assembly consisted of three groups, known as "estates." The first estate was the clergy, the second the nobil-

ity, and the third the commoners. (The term "fourth estate," which is used to describe journalism, has its roots here.)

These estates did not get along. During meetings, the first and second estates began to congregate on the right side of the chamber; the third estate tended to sit on the left. This ad hoc arrangement became the norm over the course of the Revolution.

As one might expect, the clergy and nobility—the right—were pretty happy with the way things were: They were conservative toward change to the status quo. By contrast, the commoners—the left—were tired of suffering at the hands of the wealthy: They were liberal toward change.

This ideological bifurcation was brought to the English-speaking world's attention in Thomas Carlyle's popular 1837 treatise on the French Revolution. It was soon adopted by political pundits in Britain, even though Parliament had no such seating chart.

During the nineteenth century, the concept of a political right and left moved across the pond to America. It became shorthand for the conservatism we ascribe to Republicans and the liberalism with which we characterize Democrats.

The reality, of course, is more nuanced, but broadcast blowhards work best in black and white.

Q Why didn't the Vikings stay in North America?

A Because they weren't particularly good guests, and the Native Americans threw them out. According to ancient Norse sagas that were written in the thirteenth century, Leif Eriksson was the first Viking to set foot in North America. After wintering at the place we now call Newfoundland in the year 1000, Leif went home. In 1004, his brother Thorvald led the next expedition, comprised of thirty men, and met the natives for the first time. The Vikings attacked and killed eight of the nine native men they encountered. A greater force retaliated, and Thorvald was killed. His men then returned home.

Six years later, a larger expedition of Viking men, women, and livestock set up shop in North America. They lasted two years, according to the sagas. The Vikings traded with the locals initially, but they soon started fighting with them and were driven off. There may have been one further attempt at a Newfoundland settlement by Leif and Thorvald's sister, Freydis.

In 1960, Norse ruins of the appropriate age were found in L'Anse aux Meadows, Newfoundland, by Norwegian couple Helge and Anne Stine Ingstad. The Vikings had been there, all right. Excavations over the next seven years uncovered large houses and ironworks where nails and rivets were made, as well as woodworking areas. Also found were spindlewhorls, weights that were used when spinning thread; this implies that women were present, which suggests the settlement was more than a vacation camp.

The ruins don't reveal why the Vikings left, but they do confirm what the old sagas claimed: The Vikings were in North America.

The sagas say that the settlers fought with the local *Skraelings,* a Norse word meaning "natives," until the *Skraelings* came at them in large enough numbers to force the Vikings out.

This sounds plausible, given the reputation of the Vikings—they'd been raiding and terrorizing Europe for centuries—and the Eriksson family's history of violence. Erik the Red, the father of Leif, founded a Greenland colony because he'd been thrown out of Iceland for murder, and Erik's father had been expelled from Norway for the same reason. Would you want neighbors like them?

Q Whatever happened to train cabooses?

A Like record players, beepers, and the original Yoda puppet, cabooses have been supplanted by slicker technology. But from the 1850s to the 1970s, they served an essential purpose.

Conductors on the earliest trains—made up of a mixture of passenger and freight cars—could stay in a rear passenger car to watch for any problems with the back of the train. But when the railways began to run separate passenger and freight lines in the 1850s, the freight conductor needed a new vantage point. Old boxcars were converted into conductor's cars, which were placed at the end of the train and eventually came to be known as cabooses. Passenger trains didn't usually have cabooses because the conductor could do his job just as well from a passenger car.

By the end of the nineteenth century, cabooses were standard equipment. Most included the distinctive cupola, a lookout perch extending from the top of the train. The cupola—and bay windows in later caboose designs—gave the conductor a good view of the cars ahead. A typical caboose also had a desk, a stove, and bunks for long trips.

But caboose crews weren't lounging in their bunks or looking out the windows at the amber waves of grain—they had to deal with a host of problems. For example, if a coupling failed, leaving the train in two sections, the conductor had to hit the brakes in the caboose to bring the tail section to a halt. Hotboxes (overheated axle bearings) were another common issue, requiring the crew to stop the train and replace the malfunctioning parts.

The caboose crew also operated track switches and relayed critical information for the delicate process of starting up the train. When a long train starts moving from a dead stop, it has to proceed slowly or else the cars will jerk loose from each other. As the engine creeps along, it gradually tightens the slack in the couplings between cars. In the old days, the engineer relied on the conductor in the caboose to alert him that the entire train was in motion and it was okay to "turn on the juice."

By the 1980s, most freight trains didn't need cabooses anymore thanks to new monitoring systems like the flashing rear-end device (FRED), a box attached to the back of the last car. The FRED monitors train movement and air-brake pressure and transmits this information to the train engine via radio. Similarly, electronic sensors along the sides of tracks check for hotboxes and other mechanical problems.

But the caboose didn't immediately fade away in the face of this new technology. In 1982, the United Transportation Union, which represented rail workers, agreed to lift its requirement that all freight trains have a caboose, but for several more years, many states still required it as a safety precaution. It cost railways about $1,300 per trip to operate a caboose and about eighty thousand dollars to replace one. Nostalgia couldn't compete with economic reality, and freight companies switched to the FREDs for nearly all trips as soon as it was legal. By 1990, the caboose had reached the end of the line.

Q Where did the idea for the weekend come from?

A According to the Book of Genesis, the answer is simple: The idea came from God, who rested on the seventh day after creating the universe during the previous six. But the weekend as we know it—mounting giddiness after lunch on Friday; two days of sports, yard work, and beer; and zombified Monday-morning staring—is a relatively recent development.

The ancient Jews introduced the concept of non-work at the end of the week. Their time was structured around observing the Sabbath, or Shabbat, as a day of rest and worship. In ancient Rome, the seven-day week was officially adopted in AD 321, and the early Christians chose Sunday as their Sabbath.

The weekend as a time for chilling out—with worship optional—started taking shape in Britain during its industrial revolution. In the early eighteen hundreds, large numbers of people moved to cities and into factory jobs; they logged a six-day work week, and Sunday was their official day off. In this new economy, regular people could earn enough to enjoy leisure time. That led to party-ing on Saturday evening and through most of Sunday. In the mid-eighteen hundreds, workers began taking Monday off occasion-ally to, among other things, sleep off their Sunday drunkenness. Since so many people were skipping work on Monday, and it was taboo to stage public events on the Christian Sabbath, Monday became a day for sporting events, festivals, and performances.

Religious groups weren't happy that Sunday had become a day of general debauchery. Neither were factory owners, who couldn't count on sufficient numbers of workers showing up on Monday. So, in the 1870s, many factories turned Saturday into a half day. In effect, management struck a deal with workers: We'll reduce the workload so that we can count on you showing up.

Religious groups were pleased, too: Workers could get more par-tying out of their systems on Saturday, which tipped Sunday back into the worship category. The *Oxford English Dictionary* traces the first known description of this day and a half as a "week-end" to an 1879 issue of the English magazine *Notes and Queries*.

"Week-ends" also caught on in the United States, and in 1908, a New England spinning mill changed Saturday to a full holiday so that Jewish workers could observe Shabbat. The custom spread and gained a foothold in 1926 when Henry Ford adopted it at his automobile plants. Ford wasn't just being a nice guy: More leisure time meant more travel, which meant more auto sales.

The Great Depression solidified the two-day weekend: A five-day work week divided the available jobs among more people and, thus, reduced unemployment. If only they could have squeezed an extra day of leisure in there.

Chapter Ten

WEIRD SCIENCE AND TECHNOLOGY

Q How far do you have to dive underwater to escape gunfire?

A Unlike outrunning an explosion, this action-hero escape plan actually works. A 2005 episode of the Discovery Channel's *MythBusters* proved that bullets fired into the water at an angle will slow to a safe speed at fewer than four feet below the surface. In fact, bullets from some high-powered guns in this test basically disintegrated on the water's surface.

It might seem counterintuitive that speeding bullets don't penetrate water as easily as something slow, like a diving human being or a falling anchor. But it makes sense. Water has considerable mass, so when anything hits it, it pushes back. The force of the impact is equal to the change in momentum (momentum is velocity multiplied by mass) divided by the time taken to change the momentum.

In other words, the faster the object is going, the more its momentum will change when it hits, and the greater the force of impact will be. For the same reason that a car suffers more damage in a head-on collision with a wall at fifty miles per hour than at five miles per hour, a speeding bullet takes a bigger hit than something that is moving more slowly.

The initial impact slows the bullet considerably, and the drag that's created when it moves through water brings it to a stop. The impact on faster-moving bullets is even greater, so they are more likely to break apart or slow to a safe speed within the first few feet of water.

The worst-case scenario is if someone fires a low-powered gun at you straight down into the water. In the *MythBusters* episode, one of the tests involved firing a nine-millimeter pistol directly down into a block of underwater ballistics gel. Eight feet below the surface seemed to be the safe distance—the ballistics gel showed that the impact from the bullet wouldn't have been fatal at this depth. But if a shot from the same gun were fired at a thirty-degree angle (which would be a lot more likely if you were fleeing from shooters on shore), you'd be safe at just four feet down.

The problem with this escape plan is that you have to pop up sooner or later to breathe, and the shooter on shore will be ready. But if you are a proper action hero, you can hold your breath for at least ten minutes, which is plenty of time to swim to your top-secret submarine car.

Q Why aren't all gas caps on the same side of the car?

A Your uncle's 1956 Chevy hid it behind the left taillight. On your dad's '65 Mustang, it was above the back license plate and beneath the galloping-horse emblem. Today's BMW has it on the right rear fender. Drive a Honda? Check the left rear fender. Own a Ford? It's on the right. Unless it's a Ford Fusion; then it's on the left.

We're talking gas caps, and they are no longer at the very back of the car because the fuel tank is no longer at the very back of the car. It's in front of the rear axle, protected from harm in a crash, and its filler neck enters from the side. But why isn't it on the same side from car to car?

Some speculate that it's always opposite the exhaust pipe to prevent fires from dribbled gas. Not true, say automotive designers; some cars, after all, have exhaust outlets on both sides. Another notion suggests that caps face the shoulder of the road so that luckless motorists needn't stand in traffic to refill a car that's run out of gas. But some cars from countries that drive on the right side of the road, like the United States, have left-side caps. And some cars from left-side-drive countries, like Japan and England, have right-side caps. A few optimistic souls even believe that automakers alternate sides so that we don't all queue up in the same line at the gas pump. They're mistaken.

For its part, the National Highway Traffic Safety Administration doesn't care which side the cap's on, as long as the car meets standards designed to reduce deaths and injuries from fires caused by fuel spillage during and after crashes. Tests set precise limits on the volume of fuel that can be spilled during rollovers and in rear impacts at specific rates of speed.

How automakers satisfy the requirements is their own affair. Once designers have a tank and filler neck that meet the standards, something they call "packaging" determines on which side the cap goes. Designers must route the filler neck around the suspension and exhaust components, trunk cavity, wheel housings, and door cutouts—all the stuff in the tail of a modern automobile.

Some manufacturers, like BMW and Honda, engineer all of their cars to standardize the cap on the same side. Others, like Ford and General Motors, follow the packaging dictates of each individual car. Some of today's fuel gauges display a little arrow telling us which side the cap is on. Sure, it's nice, but it's no galloping horse.

Q Can you avoid injury by jumping at the instant a falling elevator hits bottom?

A Nope—it wouldn't make much of a difference. You would be falling too rapidly to significantly lessen the impact with a jump.

As an elevator car descends, whether it is operating normally or hurtling down the shaft, gravity is continually pulling you downward, just as it does everywhere else on the planet. You are falling, and the elevator floor is the only thing that is slowing your descent.

So if you were in an elevator car that was plummeting uncontrollably, gravity would cause you to accelerate at the same rate as the car. In fact, if the elevator car were in a true free fall, you would be plummeting completely independent of the elevator, just as if you had jumped down an empty shaft. If you pushed off the floor, you would appear to be floating in midair. How's that for scary?

But here's the good news: The elevator wouldn't actually accelerate to a free fall, due to the resistance between the elevator car and the sides of the shaft, as well as resistance from the air being compressed in the shaft below. The actual speed would depend on the elevator design and the duration of the fall.

For the sake of argument, let's pretend that you are in an elevator that hits bottom while going sixty miles per hour. In order to avoid slamming into the floor at sixty miles per hour, you have to jump upward at sixty miles per hour (eighty-eight feet per second), at just the right moment so that your velocity relative to the ground is zero. The bottom line at the bottom? A two-foot vertical leap isn't going to help much.

The leading view is that you are better off lying flat on the floor, with your arms and hands around your head. The idea is to disperse the force from the impact over your whole body rather than take the full brunt of the force at any one point. Presumably, if you were standing when the elevator hit, you would fall over and possibly slam your head into the floor; if you were lying on the floor and the elevator car fell apart, you would be less likely to get whacked in the head. And with any luck, you would be in good enough shape to crawl out and limp directly to your lawyer's office.

Q What makes super glue stickier than regular glue?

A The short answer is that super glue forms an actual chemical bond between molecules, while the stickiness in normal glue is caused by much weaker attractions between molecules.

Any glue—from the stuff you used (and sometimes ate) in kindergarten to the space-age super glue that's stuck to the bottom of your junk drawer—has two types of stickiness. It needs to be adhesive, meaning that the molecules stick to other material. It also needs to be cohesive, meaning that the molecules stick to each other.

In primitive kindergarten glue, the adhesion and cohesion depend on a set of phenomena known as the van der Waals forces—weak, attractive, or repulsive forces that arise between molecules. (That vowel-heavy name is courtesy of Johannes Diderik van der Waals, the Dutch scientist who proposed the existence of intermolecular forces in the 1870s.) These forces include the attraction between adjoining molecules caused by slight differences in electrical charges on either side of each molecule.

The van der Waals forces can make the molecules of regular glue adhere and cohere, but only weakly. There's no chemical reaction to interlace the molecules and create a truly durable bond. But if there's no chemical reaction, what's going on when regular glue dries and hardens? Good question. Regular glue is a liquid because it's an emulsion of a sticky compound in water. When glue is in a bottle, the water molecules keep the compound molecules flowing so that they can't stick firmly together. But when you squirt the glue out of the bottle and expose it to air, the water evaporates. The remaining molecules of the sticky compound cling together and to any other dry material that the glue touches, making things stick to each other.

Super glue is based on an entirely different principle: a chemical reaction that forms chemical bonds. The main ingredient in super glue is cyanoacrylate, a chemical compound that polymerizes when exposed to water. In other words, the hydrogen and oxygen atoms in water enable the cyanoacrylate molecules to form chemical bonds with one another. These molecules bind together and to whatever they're touching, forming a hard plastic. These chemical bonds are much stronger than the van der Waals attractions between molecules in normal glue.

The little bit of moisture on most surfaces is enough to trigger this reaction, which is why super glue sets so quickly on just about anything. This is also why it's much more dangerous to eat super glue than regular glue: It will form a hard plastic in your body. So if you're so in touch with your inner child that you can't resist tasting glue now and then, you should stick to standard paste.

Q Is there a way to make ocean water drinkable?

A Water in the twenty-first century will be like oil was in the twentieth century: a precious, limited commodity that everybody needs and that is capable of driving nations to war. The difference is, the stakes will be even higher. You think living a week without gasoline would be tough? Try living a week without water. You'd be toast.

The United Nations estimates that by 2025, two-thirds of the world's population will not have access to adequate amounts of drinking water. Our "blue planet" is covered by vast oceans, but the freshwater we need for drinking makes up only a fraction of all the water. For various reasons, that supply of freshwater is dwindling.

In light of the looming water crisis, it seems ludicrous that we can't find a way to make those giant oceans drinkable. The good news is, we can; the not-so-good news is, it's expensive, and the impact on the environment is unknown.

Desalination (the process of removing salt from seawater) is not a new idea. Nearly two thousand years ago, crafty sailors distilled freshwater from seawater by boiling the seawater and collecting the runoff from the resulting vapor. (This is similar to the way nature creates fresh rainwater from ocean water.) But distillation on a large scale requires ridiculous amounts of energy (and, in turn, costs a ridiculous amount of money).

A cheaper method of desalination is reverse osmosis, which involves pushing seawater through a membrane that filters out the salt. The energy cost for reverse osmosis is still about ten times higher than that of treating normal freshwater, but encouraging developments that can make the process more cost-effective are ongoing.

One other issue threatens the viability of large-scale desalination: How do we dispose of all of the leftover salt concentrate? A workable answer to that question has yet to emerge. Nevertheless, desalination is hardly a pie-in-the-sky solution to the planet's looming water woes. Approximately fifteen thousand desalination plants are in operation around the world, in places like California, Florida, the Middle East, and North Africa.

These plants provide significantly less than 1 percent of the planet's drinking water, so worldwide success is still a long way off. But we remain confident that the same civilization that proudly brought us the Clapper and the Hummer Limo can find a way to prevent us from dying of thirst.

Q How does the clock on your cell phone automatically adjust when you enter a different time zone?

A Your nonstop flight to Chicago takes off from Boston at 7:25 AM. When you touch down at O'Hare Airport two hours and forty-five minutes later, you glance at your cell phone's clock and note that it's only 9:10. You've arrived just in time for your 9:30 meeting. How did your cell phone know Chicago is in the central time zone and automatically set itself back an hour from eastern time in Boston?

Cell phones receive signals from towers on the ground. As you move out of range of one tower, your phone seeks out a connection with another. In Chicago, your cell phone connects to your phone service carrier's nearest tower and receives the correct information from there, automatically updating the time.

However, the system isn't foolproof. If, after you leave your meeting, you rent a car and drive across the state border into Indiana to visit relatives, your cell phone might tell you that you have arrived just in time for lunch at 1:00 PM, but your cousin will say, "Sorry, you missed the tuna casserole." Most of Indiana is in the eastern time zone, so it's 2:00 PM for them and the food is gone. Why didn't your cell phone know that? Because the nearest tower is in Illinois and your phone is picking up a signal from there.

Techno-geeks are constantly coming up with improvements for automatic time zone adjustments on cell phones and other mobile wireless devices. One of the most recent is a "wireless synchronous time system with solar-powered transceiver," patented in 2008 by a team of six inventors from Primex Inc. in Lake Geneva, Wisconsin.

Perhaps these new solar-powered devices will bring technology full circle. With a few computerized tweaks, we will again be able to use the sun to tell time, just as our ancestors did hundreds of years ago.

Q Does my radio use more electricity when I increase the volume?

A Keeping your radio at a whisper won't save you much money, but, yes, electricity consumption does climb as you crank up the volume. When you turn the volume knob, you are increasing the electric current that is moving through an amplification circuit.

A radio broadcast is a fluctuating electrical signal that represents sound waves (fluctuations in air pressure). The radio's job is to turn this electrical signal into sound by moving a speaker cone in and out. But the original signal is too weak to drive the speaker. So the radio uses an amplifier to create a more powerful version of the signal.

The essential component that makes this possible is a bipolar transistor. On the outside of a bipolar transistor, there are three terminals: an emitter terminal, a base terminal, and a collector terminal. Inside there are layers of semiconductors, materials that conduct electricity well in some conditions and poorly in other conditions. In a bipolar transistor, the electrons in the semiconductor layers naturally arrange themselves so that the semiconductors are very poor conductors. But applying voltage to the base terminal causes the electrons to rearrange themselves so that they can conduct electricity from the collector terminal to the emitter terminal. As you increase the voltage, the transistor's conductivity increases.

The upshot is that the transistor lets you use a relatively weak current in an input circuit (connected to the collector and base terminals) to control a much greater current in an output circuit (connected to the emitter and collector terminals). In the most basic radio amplifier, the input circuit carries the broadcast signal and the output circuit is connected to the radio battery and the speaker. (In actuality, audio amplifiers include a series of these individual transistor set-ups to boost the signal a little bit at a time before passing it on to the speaker, but the principle is the same.)

Simply put, the fluctuating broadcast signal varies the resistance on the circuit connecting the battery to the speaker, causing the speaker cone to move in and out in sync with the audio signal. You control the volume in this type of circuit by turning the volume knob, which is connected to a variable resistor called a potentiometer. The classic potentiometer consists of a half-circle curved resistor and a movable wiper that slides along it. Turning the volume knob moves the wiper, which changes the length of the resistor the current must flow through. In other words, it can change the resistance in the circuit. The potentiometer typically sits in the input circuit, between amplification transistors. When you turn up the volume, the wiper moves to decrease the size of the resistor and greater voltage is applied to the base of the transistor. As a result, the transistor conducts more current in the output circuit, which means total power consumption goes up.

Don't let all of this techno-chatter stop you from rockin' out, though. Life is short, and batteries are cheap.

Q Can you play catch with the nuclear football?

A Don't start practicing your Heisman moves just yet. You could try to play catch with the nuclear football, but you'd probably throw your back out. That's because it's less like a traditional pigskin football and more like—actually, exactly like—a forty-five-pound leather-clad metal briefcase that belongs to the president of the United States. It contains crucial information and plans that the president would need in the event of a nuclear war. No matter

where the president goes, the football is always within easy reach.

The nuclear football first became a presidential accessory during the administration of John F. Kennedy. Shortly after the Cuban missile crisis, it became regrettably apparent that the president should always be prepared to respond to a nuclear attack. The president doesn't have to carry the football personally, of course; that job is handled by a rotating staff of five military aides.

Officially known as the president's emergency satchel, its nickname originated with one of the government's early nuclear war plans, which was code-named "Dropkick." It is said to carry a secure satellite phone that can connect the president to the Pentagon and two emergency command centers that are bunkered in the mountains of Colorado and Pennsylvania. Other goodies include war plans, activation codes for launching nuclear weapons, and guidelines for where in the country the president should go during an emergency.

If you really did manage to play catch with the nuclear football, you'd probably barely even notice the pain in your back. You'd likely be much more focused on the gang of angry Secret Service agents pummeling you into submission.

Q How do they get stripes in toothpaste?

A Who says we at F.Y.I. headquarters are afraid to delve into the important, life-changing stuff? There are two methods for packaging striped toothpaste, and we boldly plan to tell you about each.

Some manufacturers pump two or three colors of toothpaste into the tube at the same time, side by side. The stripes might come out of the tube a bit messy, since the colors can mix together during squeezing, but for the most part, this method works fine. The paste is thick and packed tightly into the tube, so it won't mix too much.

The other method is to add an extension to the toothpaste nozzle. This extension is basically a plastic straw that extends an inch or so down from the nozzle into the tube. The straw has two small holes on the sides, near the nozzle opening. First, the manufacturer adds a small amount of colored paste into the tube—just enough to surround the straw; then it fills the rest of the tube with white paste and seals the tube at the end.

When you squeeze the end of the tube, the pressure pushes white paste out through the middle of the straw and forces the colored paste through the two smaller holes, adding the colored stripes just before the paste leaves the nozzle. Since the colored paste and white paste don't mix until they are coming out of the tube, everything comes out with perfect stripes.

Does striped toothpaste serve a real purpose? Of course not—it's just a marketing gimmick. Toothpaste includes different ingredients, but they don't need to be different colors or separated. Consumers have the final word on this one, and they have spoken: When Aquafresh came out in the 1970s, it quickly rose to third place in the toothpaste market—thanks, in part, to its pretty stripes.

Q How do fireworks form different shapes?

A Fireworks have been delighting people (and on the negative side, blowing off fingers) for more than seven hundred years, and the design hasn't changed much in that time. Getting those fireworks to form complex shapes is one of the trickier challenges, but the basic idea is still fairly old school.

To understand what's involved, it helps to know some fireworks basics. A fireworks shell is a heavy paper container that holds three sections of explosives. The first section is the "lift charge," a packet of black powder (a mixture of potassium nitrate, sulphur, and charcoal) at the bottom of the shell. To prepare the shell for launch, a pyrotechnician places the shell in a mortar (a tube that has the same diameter as the shell), with the lift charge facing downward. A quick-burning fuse runs from the lift charge to the top of the mortar. To fire the shell, an electric trigger lights the quick fuse. It burns down to ignite the black powder at the bottom of the shell, and the resulting explosion propels the shell out of the mortar and high into the air.

The second explosive section is the "bursting charge," a packet of black powder in the middle of the shell. When the electric trigger lights the quick-burning fuse, it also lights a time-delay fuse that runs to the bursting charge. As the shell is hurtling through the air, the time-delay fuse is burning down. Around the time the shell reaches its highest point, the fuse burns down to the bursting charge, and the black powder explodes.

Expanding black powder isn't exactly breathtaking to watch. The vibrant colors you see come from the third section of explosives, known as the "stars." Stars are simply solid clumps of explosive metals that emit colored light when they burn. For example, burning copper salts emit blue light and burning barium nitrate emits green light. The expanding black powder ignites the stars and propels them outward, creating colored streaks in the sky.

The shape of the explosion depends on how the manufacturer positions the stars in the shell. To make a simple ring, it places the stars in a ring around the bursting charge; to make a heart, it positions the stars in a heart shape. Manufacturers can make more complex fireworks patterns, such as a smiley face, by combining multiple compartments with separate bursting charges and stars in a single shell. As the fuse burns, these different "breaks" go off in sequence. In a smiley face shell, the first break that explodes makes a ring, the second creates two dots for the eyes, and the third forms a crescent shape for the mouth.

It's hard to produce designs that are much more complex than that, since only a few breaks can be set off in quick succession. So if you're hoping to see a fireworks tribute to origami, you're out of luck.

Q If you use a stun gun on someone and he grabs you, will you get stunned too?

A Everyone knows that electricity from power lines and lightning can pass through your body and fry you in the process. So if the human body is such a good conductor of electricity, why wouldn't you stun yourself if you zapped a mugger and he grabbed hold of you?

Simple: Stun guns simply aren't powerful enough. The purpose of a stun gun isn't to zap the entire body, but rather to use just enough voltage (typically about fifty thousand volts) to send a low-level electrical charge (around three milliamps) as far as the nearest nerve. This usually doesn't do any permanent damage; it just disrupts the nervous system.

Your brain transmits messages to the muscles in your body by conducting electrical signals through your nerves. Zapping someone is like interfering with a radio signal by broadcasting another signal at the same frequency. The original messages from the brain, which are telling the muscles to move in particular ways, are garbled by the electrical interference from a stun gun.

Since all of the human body's nerves are interconnected, you can zap someone anywhere and the signal will trigger involuntary muscle contractions all over. But once the electrical jolt is in the nervous system, the charge dissipates and doesn't have enough voltage to jump to anyone else. So if you ever get mugged, feel free to use your stun gun with impunity.

Q How does scratch-and-sniff stuff work?

A The basic idea is simple: Manufacturers encase tiny drops of scented oil in thin polymer membranes and stick millions of these little bitty capsules to a piece of paper or a sticker. When you scratch the paper, your fingernail breaks open the tiny capsules and the scented oil (along with its smell) spills out. And there you have it—instant banana odor.

The manufacturing process—called microencapsulation—is a little more complicated. To whip up a batch of scratch-and-sniff stuff, manufacturers combine scented oil and a solution of water and a polymer compound in a big vat. The oil and the solution won't mix, just like oil and vinegar in vinaigrette salad dressing won't mix. But when a giant blending machine stirs everything, the oil breaks down into millions of tiny drops that are suspended in the polymer solution. You see the same effect when you shake a bottle of vinaigrette.

Next the manufacturer adds a catalyst chemical to the mix that reacts with the polymer and changes its behavior. While before it was soluble (it dissolved in water), in its new form it becomes insoluble (it doesn't mix with water). In other words, the polymer separates from the water and turns into a solid. As it solidifies, it forms shells around the tiny oil droplets. The manufacturer dries these capsules and mixes them into a slurry, so that they can be applied to scratch-and-sniff strips.

It's yet another example of how science is being put to good use and making the world a better place for one and all.

Chapter Eleven

ORIGINS

Q **How much room do you need to swing a cat?**

A Quarters are tight here in the F.Y.I. war room. Towers of folders that are overflowing with archival research teeter dangerously over our postage-stamp-size desks, where we slave away amongst a heady blend of ink, paper, and each other. It's not pleasant. Anyway, in our cramped office, the following phrase is frequently muttered with dismay: "There's not enough room in here to swing a cat." And that got us wondering: Just how much room might one need to accomplish the task?

To answer this question, we need to trace the phrase's origin. There are multiple theories, and, no, they have nothing to do with the Jazz Age and all of its swingin' cats. Furthermore, according to the first explanation, the phrase might not even have anything to do with felines. It seems that back in the seventeenth and eighteenth centuries, any sailor in the British navy who misbehaved was rewarded with a flogging with a whip that featured nine knotted lashes. This menacing little device was known as a "cat o' nine tails." Because a great deal of open space was required for the whip to be used effectively—and because floggings were frequently done in view of other sailors as a lesson—the old cat o' nine tails was only broken out in a spacious area, such as the poop deck.

A second camp argues that the phrase originated in a medieval archery game in which a cat was put into a leather bag and swung from the nearest tree or rafter and used for target practice. This theory has some weaknesses, not the least of which is determining a conceivable reason for archers to practice so cruelly. There is also little historical evidence to back up this claim, though in Shakespeare's *Much Ado About Nothing,* the cantankerous Benedick says, "If I do, hang me in a bottle like a cat and shoot at me; and he that hits me, let him be clapped on the shoulder, and called Adam."

Neither of these theories seems to indicate that there was ever a time when people were swinging actual felines by the tail. But what if you wanted to? It seems clear that swinging a cat requires space, but just how much? Fortunately, we remember our geometry. Let's say that the average cat is about twenty-four inches long and that the tail is about twelve inches long. We also need space for our arms, and the average human male's arms are twenty-eight inches long.

That means we'll need sixty-four inches, or more than five feet of swinging radius. Recalling our handy little formula for the area of a circle, we know that the total area required is 12,867 inches. Of course, most rooms aren't circular. The area of a square room with sides of 128 inches (the diameter of our circle) is about 114 square feet.

In other words, a space far, far larger than our office.

Q Who decided it was okay for women to wear pants?

A Think of a political firebrand who encourages women everywhere to cast off the constricting bonds of man-pleasing fashion. If you're imagining a throwback to the 1960s, you're on the right track—but forget the bra-burning feminists of the hippie era and go back more than a hundred years earlier. Sure, the garments were a little different—corsets were undoubtedly trickier to set aflame—but the sentiment was the same. And for these early feminists, there was a simple wardrobe solution: pants.

One of the leaders of this cause was Amelia Jenks Bloomer, a reformer who was present when the women's suffrage movement was born at the Seneca Falls Convention in 1848. The following year, Bloomer established a newspaper for women called *The Lily: A Monthly Journal, Devoted to Temperance and Literature.* Sometime around 1851, Bloomer began advocating dress reform from the pages of her influential journal. She encouraged women to eschew the whalebone corsets, petticoats, heavy skirts, and other cumbersome garments that were then in vogue. To show that she meant business, she began making public appearances in full-cut pantaloons, also known as Turkish trousers, which she wore under a shorter skirt.

Bloomer wasn't the first woman to don this scandalous style. Others, including actress Fanny Kemble (the Lindsay Lohan of her day) had rocked Turkish trou even earlier. But because of Bloomer's high-profile promotion of the garment, they came to be known popularly as "bloomers." The name caught on, but the look didn't. Bloomer was often ridiculed for wearing her bloomers, and even prominent members of the women's movement soon abandoned the style because they felt that it was doing their cause more harm than good.

It wasn't until the next century that pants became a respectable fashion choice for women. Hollywood stars like Marlene Dietrich and Katharine Hepburn began wearing pants in 1930s, and by 1939, *Vogue* magazine was insisting that slacks were a fashion essential.

But back to Bloomer, the pioneer of women's pants. She wanted nothing more than to improve the United States—she boldly advocated temperance and equal rights for women. But unfortunately, her legacy resides in those preposterous eponymous pantaloons.

Q What does staying sober have to do with being on the wagon?

A Plenty. The phrase "on the wagon" likely originated in America sometime in the late nineteenth century, a period of fervent campaigning for temperance and prohibition. With breweries and saloons popping up everywhere, organizations like the Woman's Christian Temperance Union, the Anti-Saloon League, and the Total Abstinence Society actively encouraged husbands and fathers to stay sober and out of trouble.

"I promise to abstain from all intoxicating drinks, except used medicinally and by order of a medical man, and to discountenance the cause and practice of intemperance," went the pledge of the Total Abstinence Society. Millions of people took it, and they were then considered to be "on the water cart."

Why, you ask? At that time, horse-drawn water carts were common sights in U.S. cities. They weren't used to distribute drinking water, but to wet down the dusty roads during hot, dry weather. So the metaphor "I'm on the water cart" really came from this sort of sentiment: "Sure, I'm thirsty for a beer, but I'd rather take a drink from that old dusty water cart than break my solemn vow."

The earliest literary citation of "on the water cart" likely can be found in Alice Caldwell Hegan's 1901 comic novel *Mrs. Wiggs of the*

Cabbage Patch: "I wanted to git him some whisky, but he shuck his head. 'I'm on the water-cart,' sez he." After that, the popular American idiom evolved into "on the water wagon" and then simply into "on the wagon." But regardless of whether it's a cart or a wagon, we all know just how easy it is to fall off.

Q Why would you want to open a can of worms?

A Back in the 1950s, bait shops sold worms in old tin cans. A fisherman would buy a can of worms and fasten a piece of wood on the top as a lid. When he got to his fishing hole, he opened the can to get a worm. If he forgot to put the lid back on, he might find himself short of bait. Why? Well, as they say, "The worms crawl in, the worms crawl out." They also crawl around and about, disappearing quickly into the earth. Rounding up the worms once they're out of the can is a futile process, as any frustrated fisherman can tell you.

Don't open a can of worms unless you want to see things get out of hand. For instance, at Thanksgiving dinner, your mom might whisper, "Don't open that can of worms" when you insist on asking ultraconservative Uncle Fred how he voted in the last election. Or perhaps your boss admonishes, "We're not opening that can of worms" when your colleague pipes up at the staff meeting with, "Who's getting a Christmas bonus this year?"

On the other hand, if you like riling people, you might want to consider a career as a professional can o' worms opener. Investigative reporters get paid to pry into secrets and stir up trouble.

In the summer of 1972, Bob Woodward and Carl Bernstein of the *Washington Post* set out to discover who had broken into the Democratic Party headquarters in the Watergate complex. By the time they were done, Richard Nixon had become the first United States president in history to resign. Not bad for two cub reporters who were opening their first can of worms.

Believe it or not, it's still possible to buy real cans of worms, though they're more likely to come in a plastic bucket than a tin cylinder. *EarthWorm Digest,* which bills itself as "The #1 Earthworm Information Website in the World," offers agriculturists a complete guide to vermiculture. A thousand red worms will run you between twenty and thirty bucks, plus shipping costs. Turn them loose in your compost heap, and within a couple of years, you might have hundreds of thousands of hardworking worms stirring up rich, nutritious fertilizer for your garden.

So whether you're aiming for a Pulitzer Prize or a crop of prize tomatoes, there are occasions when opening up a can of worms can be a good thing.

Q What was so great about the salad days?

A There's nothing quite like the memory of our salad days. It was the time when we were innocent, before we learned of life and love, when Thousand Island dressing flowed like water. Wait, what? Okay, we've just been informed that Thousand Island dressing has nothing to do with the salad days. Well, then what *was* so great about the salad days?

Shakespeare himself coined the phrase. This shouldn't come as a surprise; scholars of the Bard can list well more than a thousand words and phrases that we owe to his plays. Of course, when you've got so many ideas, some are bound to be duds. And even though "salad days" is still a popular expression after four hundred years, it's not one of Billy S.'s finer efforts.

He introduced the phrase in *Antony and Cleopatra,* when Cleo uses it to dismiss a reminder of her long-ago crush on that dreamboat Julius Caesar. Yeah, I totally hooked up with him, she essentially says, but only because I was young and naïve, and he had a bitchin' chariot. Those were "my salad days, when I was green in judgment: cold in blood." This doesn't make a heck of a lot of sense until you realize that Shakespeare is making a play on words. He likens the metaphorical "greenness" of inexperienced youth to the literal greenness of the fresh veggies in a cool, crisp salad. Hence, the days of naïvete and innocence become "salad days," a miserable play on words that wilts harder than a Denny's garden salad.

The phrase caught on, however, and has been used in subsequent centuries to refer to any type of youthful inexperience. But as far as we're concerned, the real salad days didn't begin until 1912, when Thousand Island dressing was invented.

Q Why are some women called "catty"?

A Just what qualifies as catlike behavior? According to the Humane Society of the United States, cats are highly territorial animals, even more so than dogs. When it comes to defending their turf, cats will hiss, swat, chase, or ambush any other feline they see as a threat.

But a cat's behavior can be pretty difficult to predict. It's not uncommon for a cat to be territorially aggressive toward one cat yet completely cordial to another. Who knows what sets off cats? One minute they're soft, purring balls of fuzz; the next they're scratching your eyes out.

Sounds a lot like the ladies at the office, huh?

Executive coach Alicia Smith says that no one ever wants to be accused of cattiness, but at one time or another, most women have probably engaged in it. She says cattiness "can include any number of unfortunate behaviors, from not saying what we really intend to say, to saying things in a harsh tone of voice. It also includes gossiping, cynical remarks, and on a grander scale, outright rudeness."

Why so much cattiness? A 2006 study on catty behavior by University of Arkansas graduate student Kristen Norwood found that women's petty, spiteful behavior is usually the result of jealousy, competition, and insecurity. The participants in Norwood's study admitted that the potential for a catty conflict— even with strangers—was frequent. And the number one reason for the dirty looks, eye rolls, and disparaging digs? Jealousy over physical attractiveness and attention from men.

"Society sets girls up to compete with each other, primarily for male attention," says Betsy Crane of the department of sociology at Indiana University of Pennsylvania. "And I think it carries over into day-to-day life." As for catty competition on the job, Crane speculates that society is still adjusting to women in the workplace. "Women are moving into a new sphere and gaining power," she says. "Through this, though, they're having to learn how to relate to each other and to men in different ways."

And you thought it all came down to PMS.

Q How did the days of the week get their names?

A Just like our language itself, the English words for the days of the week embody a hodgepodge of influences. Some of our names came from the ancient Babylonians and were retained by the Romans. The rest were coined by the Anglo-Saxons, and you have our permission to blame these Germanic settlers of fifth-century Britain for all of the times that you misspelled "Wednesday" when you were a kid.

When the Babylonians established the seven-day week, they named the first day after the sun and the second after the moon. The next five days were named for the five planets of which they were aware.

They had looked to their gods when labeling the planets, and so they named the third day of the week for Mars, the god of war; the fourth for Mercury, god of merchants and messenger of the gods; the fifth for Jupiter, god of the sky, who brought rain and lightning; the sixth for Venus, goddess of love; and the last day of the week for Saturn, god of seed. The Romans admired the

Babylonians' style. They retained the custom of days named for heavenly bodies and their representative deities, and took along their calendar on a four-hundred-year visit to England. When finally the Romans skedaddled back to Italy, in barged the Anglo-Saxons.

The Anglo-Saxons were so occupied with pillaging that they found time to rename only four of the seven days—they retained the sun, moon, and Saturn monikers. For the rest, the Anglo-Saxons, like those before them, turned to their gods. Interestingly, they endeavored to identify each of their gods with its Roman predecessor.

So for the third day of the week, the Anglo-Saxons turned to *Tiw,* their god of war. For the fourth day, they chose *Woden,* the supreme deity. The fifth day went to *Thor*, god of thunder. And the sixth was named for their god of love, *Frigg.* (Yes, Frigg.)

Variant spellings exist, but, basically, what the Anglo-Saxons called *sunnan daeg* is now Sunday. *Monan daeg* is now Monday. *Tiwes daeg* evolved into Tuesday. *Wodnes daeg* (which didn't evolve enough) became Wednesday. *Thorsdagr* is Thursday. *Frigedaeg* is Friday. And *Saeterdag* is Saturday. And you now also have our permission to declare, "Thank Frigg it's Friday!"

Q What's the difference between a dirty look and the evil eye?

A A dirty look is something you get when you tell an inappropriate joke at the dinner table or show up at church

206 · Why Won't Men Ask for Directions?

wearing a skirt that's too short. It's someone's way of telling you: "Hey, you. See this ugly look on my face? It means I don't like what you're doing. Not one bit."

When a dirty look is directed your way, you have lots of options. You can ignore it, laugh it off, shake it off, or even return it in kind. A dirty look is just a tiny, temporary moment of disapproval or disdain. You'll get over it.

Not so with the evil eye. In many cultures and religious traditions, the evil eye is thought to be such a malevolent force that it can bring about disease, injury, and even death. Talk about bad vibes. Want to avoid the curse? Steer clear of any ungainly glances from childless women, old women, and malformed individuals. According to folklore, these are the kinds of people who are most likely to harbor malice toward you because they're envious of your prosperity and beauty.

Of course, you can't really help that you were born with the looks of a model, a generous trust fund, and acres of bountiful farmland. In that case, you may need to take more protective measures against the mean-spirited misfortunes of the evil eye.

In the teachings of Kabbalah, a red string is tied around the left wrist to ward off the negative influences of unfriendly stares. In Asia, children may have their faces blackened, especially around the eyes, for protection. And in Turkey, blue "evil eye" beads that are made of glass are turned into trinkets, amulets, necklaces, bracelets, and anklets and are hung on everything from horses and babies to rearview mirrors and office doors. Hey, when it comes to the evil eye, it's better to be safe (and tacky) than sorry. Or dead.

Q What is a bad hair day?

A Sky-high frizz, little sprigs of cowlick, the comb-over that won't comb over. No magic comb, curling iron, or straightening serum can fix this tress mess. It's only 8:00 AM, but when your coif doesn't cooperate, a promising new day seems doomed. Oh, look: The cat just peed on your briefcase. What else can go wrong?

A whole lot, according to a Yale University "bad hair day" study. It seems that the effects of an unmanageable mane extend beyond what's in the mirror. The Yale research, headed by Dr. Marianne LaFrance in 2000, found a direct relationship between a bad hair day and psychological well-being.

"Interestingly, both women and men are negatively affected by the phenomenon of bad hair days," reported LaFrance. "Even more fascinating is our finding that individuals perceive their capabilities to be significantly lower than others when experiencing bad hair."

That's right—the study, commissioned by Procter & Gamble's Physique hair care line, found that bad hair lowers performance self-esteem, increases social insecurity, and intensifies self-criticism. It turns out that a bad hair day can spiral into a self-loathing, self-destructive, mangy mess of a pity party. No wonder you missed the train, spilled coffee on your boss, and dropped your keys through a drainage grate.

Well, snap out it! There's more than one way to lock down wayward locks. For starters, get the very best haircut you can afford. "It's the cut that determines how easy your hair will be to style," counsels Beverly Hills hairdresser Nick Chavez. "And a good one can go a long way in helping you avoid a bad hair day."

Next, use a shampoo and a conditioner that are designed to deal with your hair type. Got haystack hair? Go with a moisturizing formula. Your scalp is an oil slick? Get rid of the grease with an oil-controlling concoction. And there's a simple fix for staticky, flyaway, just-been-electrocuted hair: Rub it down with a dryer sheet. Bounce, Downey, Snuggle—basically, grab whatever's in the laundry room. It'll keep hair from sticking together and make styling a lot easier.

But do you know what's even simpler? A fashionable hat.

Q Why are broomsticks associated with witches?

A Brooms and witches go together like—well, let's just call it a "special relationship."

Wicca, a type of witchcraft or a "nature religion," is still very much alive today. Its practitioners are known as Wiccans. Your average twenty-first-century Wiccan—when not surfing the Web, listening to Stevie Nicks on the iPod, or chauffeuring the kids off to soccer practice in the Navigator—still uses a broom from time to time when performing the rituals of witchcraft. In addition to its handy dust-busting qualities, the broom is a tool that sweeps negativity and impurities out of areas where Wiccan rituals take place.

For hundreds of years, the broom has played this role in the practice of witchcraft. But there are some researchers who believe that the broom's original connection with witches was a little more, shall we say, personal. It's important to remember whom we're talking about here: They were witches, not Girl Scouts.

Some evidence suggests that women of yore who were accused of being witches were actually under the influence of hallucinogens. Those poor souls in Salem, Massachusetts, who were hanged in 1692 for being witches may have been reacting to a poisonous fungus called ergot that made its way into their bread. Ergot grows on rye in cool, damp weather, and when ingested, it has effects similar to those of LSD. According to this theory, the victims' ergot-inspired fits and convulsions, along with the visions they reported, were enough to freak out their neighbors and inspire accusations of witchery.

But accidental poisoning was not the only cause of hallucinations among supposed witches. Some appear to have been quite proactive in the whole affair, purposefully embarking on mind-expanding trips by consuming certain substances or by applying certain ointments. Of course, for the psychoactive ingredients in a hallucinogenic ointment to work, they have to enter the blood stream, which can only happen via the body's mucous membranes. In other words, if you don't want to eat it, you've got to put it...*down there.*

In his 1973 book *Hallucinogens and Shamanism*, Michael J. Harner documents a fourteenth-century example of this less-than-hygienic practice. It seems that a woman accused of witchcraft was known to have "greased a staffe" with ointment and administered said "staffe" to a certain lady-specific part of her body, with rousing results. According to this line of thinking, a witch's broomstick may have originally served the same purpose as the "staffe"—a handy applicator for hallucinogenic drugs. And what better way to escape the drudgery of housework?

Next Halloween, take a gander at those creepy green-skinned witches riding on their broomsticks, and you'll notice that they all seem to be sporting that same lascivious-looking grin...

Q Why can't you teach an old dog new tricks?

A It's not that you can't; it's that you might face some frustration if you try. As the brain ages—whether it be a canine's or a human's—it loses neurons, or nerve cells. With fewer neurons, there are fewer connections between the neurons, and it's in these connections that your memories are stored. Before you know it, you've spent over an hour looking for your bifocals when they've been on your head the whole time.

Young people run circles around old folks in terms of short-term memory, perceptual speed, muscular strength, and physical coordination. They also have much sharper vision and hearing. But that certainly doesn't mean that a Methuselah has to throw in the towel.

"Learning a new skill, like playing the piano or speaking a foreign language, would be harder at age eighty than age eight, since all bodily processes decline as we age," says Dr. Linda Espinosa, a retired professor of education who taught at the University of Missouri-Columbia. "But it's certainly not impossible."

Okay, so maybe it's too late for Gramps to master that triple Sal-chow on ice. But he did learn how to get cash from the ATM and program the VCR to tape his favorite reruns of *Matlock*. And that's pretty cool.

According to John W. Rowe and Robert K. Khan, authors of the MacArthur Foundation study "Successful Aging," research shows that "older people can, and do, learn new things—and they learn them well." But it's important to be realistic: "The limits of learn-ing, and especially the pace of learning, are more restricted in age than in youth."

Want to stay sharp as a tack well into your twilight years? Rowe and Khan say that three lifestyle features predict strong mental functions in old age: regular physical activity, a strong social sup-port system, and a belief in your ability to deal with whatever life throws at you.

That's all well and good, but where are those car keys?

Q Why would you wear your heart on your sleeve?

A Back in medieval times, a knight might have asked a fair lady for a scarf, a handkerchief, or some other token of her love before entering a jousting tournament. He tied this token around his arm so that everyone would know for whom he fought. In other words, the knight wore the sign of his love, or "heart," upon his armored sleeve for all to see.

Is wearing your heart on your sleeve a good thing? If you're up-front about your feelings, yes. When *Vogue* magazine tells us that actor Viggo Mortensen is "known for wearing his heart and his politics on his sleeve," we know that Mortensen's real-life persona is just as expressive and dramatic as that of the characters he portrays. People who wear their hearts on their sleeves come across as honest, passionate, and appealing.

Shakespeare, though, gave the words another twist. In *Othello,* arch-villain and master of deceit Iago declares, "But I will wear my heart upon my sleeve for daws to peck at." Showing your true feelings, according to Iago's devious mind, only invites criticism and gossip, embodied by the pecking "daws." He has no intention of letting Othello know his real intentions, and he displays only false friendship and loyalty, rather than his true heart, on his sleeve.

We have many ways of telling the world who or what we hold most dear. We can put our hearts on bumper stickers, lapel buttons, T-shirts, and tote bags. We can even post them on our "cyber sleeves," courtesy of MySpace and Facebook. Whether you think it's in your best interest is up to you. Remember, the romantic hero Romeo wore his heart on his sleeve, and he is one of Shakespeare's most memorable characters.

Chapter Twelve

BODY SCIENCE

Q Why are opera singers fat?

A This is what happens when your notions of the world are derived from Bugs Bunny cartoons rather than actual experience. Were you to take the bowl of pork rinds out of your lap for long enough to actually attend a performance, you'd see that most opera singers are height-and-weight proportionate. Just look at the world-famous Three Tenors: Luciano Pavarotti, Plácido Domingo, and José Carreras. The late Pavarotti is the only one you could legitimately describe as fat. Sure, Domingo could stand to lose a pound or two, but "fat" is overstating it.

Our first inclination was to scrap this seemingly silly question and spend the rest of the afternoon playing Frisbee out in the parking lot here at F.Y.I. headquarters. But out of principle, we did some initial research, which turned up a few nagging links between opera singing and weight. So much for Frisbee—it was back to the salt mines for us.

First, we stumbled across the curious case of Maria Callas, a renowned soprano from the middle part of the twentieth century. Before the age of thirty, Ms. Callas had achieved as much fame as is possible in an art form that is ignored by roughly 80 percent of the population. But at the pinnacle of her singing career, she decided to undergo a radical weight-loss regimen, presumably because it was difficult for audiences to accept her as a ravishing young maiden if she waddled out on stage looking like John Madden.

She lost more than eighty pounds in one year, leading to fantastical rumors that she had intentionally swallowed a tapeworm. Wild speculation continued to mount when her voice started to fail; many people postulated that her decreased size put an extra strain on her vocal cords and prematurely ended her career.

What does this anecdote tell us? Well, basically nothing. The conjecture about Callas's weight loss and the quality of her singing was just that: uneducated guessing. There was no definitive proof either way.

Okay, onward to exhibit B: Deborah Voigt, who was fired from a production in 2004 because the director felt that she was too heavy to fit into her costume. After such a public humiliation, many of us would opt for suicide or, at least, a Unabomber-style shack out in the woods. Ms. Voigt chose neither route—instead, she underwent gastric bypass surgery. Now, unlike our previous example, Voigt lives in a time of incessant media scrutiny and a culture obsessed with physical appearance. As a result, we are privy to endless interviews with the singer immediately following her radical weight loss and the ensuing performances.

In a 2005 interview with the *New York Times,* Voigt said, "There is no question that I have to think about my technique more than I did." Interesting, huh? She goes on to say, "The sort of automatic engagement of the abdominal muscles from the excess weight doesn't happen anymore." This last bit seems promising—at least as far as our question is concerned—but what in the name of *The Barber of Seville* does it mean? Who knows?

In the end, all we can really say is that in this one case, a particular opera singer *felt* that her weight aided her ability to sing opera. There is still no scientific evidence that links girth to singing ability. Sorry to lead you on a wild goose chase, but at least we now can break out the Frisbee with the knowledge that we tried our best.

Q Do identical twins have identical fingerprints?

A It would help many criminals if they did: Courtroom revelations of "mysterious long-lost twins" would probably skyrocket. But fortunately for law enforcement, everybody has distinct fingerprints, including two people with identical DNA.

Why? Because DNA doesn't completely dictate the way we develop. We are born the way we are because of a combination of genetics and random environmental factors in the womb. In the case of fingerprints, DNA roughly dictates how ridge patterns will be formed. In other words, genetics determines whether a fingerprint will be an arch, a whorl, a loop, or a mix of different varieties.

A variety of influences in the uterus, including how the skin contacts amniotic fluid and how the bones are grow during fingerprint formation, determine how the ridges end and split. These pattern alterations of the ridges, collectively known as minutiae, are what give you unique fingerprints. Interestingly, identical twins generally have a similar number of fingerprint minutiae and ridges, even though the patterns differ.

It's not just fingerprint patterns that grow differently. Random forces in the womb can give twins unique skin blemishes and even shape their faces differently. In fact, if one twin has a better connection to the placenta, he or she can eat better and might be significantly bigger at birth than his or her womb mate. Hey, it's never too early to get a step ahead in a sibling rivalry.

Q Why isn't my pee always the same color?

A Even if you're a paragon of health, the color of your urine changes from day to day. One morning you might warm the porcelain with pee that's the color of straw; the next you might see a tint that is reminiscent of our nation's amber waves of grain. It's all good—urologists consider anything from faint yellow to deep amber to be acceptable.

The shade of your urine generally depends on how much you've been drinking. If you've been guzzling fluids all day, a large percentage of your pee will be water and it will be almost crystal clear. But if it's been a while since you had anything to drink, your urine will appear yellowish.

Urine gets its color from derivatives of bilirubin, the yellowish-brown waste product that remains after your body has broken down old blood cells and recycled their useful pieces. To get rid of this biological garbage, your body transfers the bilirubin to your liver, which passes it through the small intestine and into the kidneys. Along the way, the bilirubin is broken down into its derivatives, which are excreted by the kidneys into the urine or the feces.

The color of your urine can say a lot about what's going on in your body. Abnormal color—anything that's not in the yellow section of the rainbow—can indicate severe internal problems. Dark brown might signal an issue with the liver or the bile ducts; red might mean internal bleeding; and black is indicative of a rare genetic disease.

Urine that's brilliant yellow, on the verge of being fluorescent, is nothing to worry about. This odd discoloration is often the result of taking too many vitamins. Riboflavin, in particular, will make your pee look like highlighter ink.

Just as you should check the fluid levels in your car's engine every so often, it's a good idea to take a gander in the toilet whenever you relieve yourself. And if you have any questions about the color of your pee, ask your body's mechanic, a.k.a. your doctor.

Q Why can Sherpas exist at higher altitudes than anyone else?

A In the early twentieth century, when Westerners first began to dream of reaching the summit of Mount Everest, one lesson quickly became clear: It was fruitless to try to make the climb without a Sherpa.

For the average person, the atmosphere way up there—29,035 feet at the mountain's peak—is not all that different from being in outer space. The thin air and extreme cold make it a deadly environment. Hypoxia, also known as mountain sickness, sets in quickly, resulting in hallucinations and impaired judgment. (We'd argue that the mere decision to attempt such a climb might be ample evidence of impaired judgment.)

But Western mountaineers on those early expeditions noticed that their Sherpa guides often seemed impervious to the dangers of high altitude. They maintained their strength and breathed the thin air with ease. The cold didn't seem to bother them, either. All in all, they were downright cheerful, even under the most dreadful conditions. So Sherpas became indispensable climbing companions. Sir Edmund Hillary, a native of New Zealand, wasn't alone when he became the first person ever to reach the summit of Everest in 1953—Tenzing Norgay, his Sherpa guide, was right behind him, "taking photographs and eating mint cake," as Norgay later described it.

In 1963, after the first American expedition reached the summit, three climbers were unable to complete the descent of the mountain because of frostbite, and they had to be rescued by Sherpas. Teams of four Sherpas carried each man for two days. The climbers later reported that by the end of the first day, their Sherpa rescuers not only were unaffected, but they had even become competitive, racing each other back to base camp.

What makes Sherpas so special? The Sherpa people are a small ethnic group concentrated in the Himalayan regions of Nepal, India, and Tibet. About ten thousand of them live in the Khumbu Valley of Mount Everest at elevations of about ten to twelve thousand feet. The reasons for their resistance to the dangerous effects of high altitude remain a mystery. Some researchers believe that living in high-altitude villages for hundreds of years has created an inherent genetic predisposition in Sherpas that allows them to cope with the rarefied air.

Whatever the reason, the message is obvious: Always take a Sherpa with you on the way up Everest, and be sure to pack enough mint cake for everybody.

Q Can someone read your mind?

A *Develop Your ESP! Unleash Your Psychic Powers!* Have you ever wanted to read someone's mind? Dozens of books promise to teach you mental telepathy in a few simple steps. Extrasensory perception, or ESP, is big business, but is it for real?

Rupert Sheldrake thinks so. He's a biochemist who was a fellow of Clare College at Britain's Cambridge University. In 2003, he published *The Sense of Being Stared At.* The title is taken from an experiment Sheldrake conducted in which he blindfolded volunteers and asked them to guess whether somebody was staring at them. Sheldrake claimed that his subjects were correct 60 percent of the time, a slightly higher score than the 50 percent suggested by the laws of probability.

In another experiment, he asked a volunteer to guess who of four people was going to contact him by phone or e-mail. Again, Sheldrake's subjects beat the odds—they were right about 40 percent of the time as opposed to the law-of-averages 25 percent.

Though intriguing, these results are hardly convincing. Most scientists believe that they can be attributed to problems that usually crop up in experiments that are based on "guessing games." In brief, few people will give the same answer each time; they'll switch around, thus increasing their chances of scoring a "hit."

In 1974, Charles Honorton and Dr. Stanley Krippner, researchers at the Maimonides Medical Center in Brooklyn, New York, designed one of the most popular tests of extrasensory perception: the Ganzfield experiment, after the German expression *ganzfeld* ("whole field"). It involved placing one volunteer in a state of sensory deprivation—eyes covered, earphones blocking sound, gloves reducing tactile sensations—while a second volunteer in another room concentrated on a picture and tried to "send" it to his or her partner. After about an hour, the first volunteer was shown four images and asked which he or she saw during sensory deprivation.

The Ganzfeld experiment was performed eighty-eight times with more than three thousand pairs of volunteers from 1974 to 2004. The subjects scored "hits" about a third of the time, above the odds but not high enough to convince skeptics that ESP was in play.

Most of what we know about mind reading comes from anecdotes, which are difficult to replicate in a lab setting. Many people engage in a form of mind reading without knowing it. Have you ever had the sense that a friend was feeling worried, even though she was smiling? Perhaps you were responding to her body language or subtle changes in her tone of voice. Human beings are social creatures and are always sending nonverbal signals to each other.

"Mind readers" often are especially adept at picking up clues about the emotional states of others. It's called empathy, and while it may not be as exciting as the notion of extrasensory perception, it's a skill that enables people to stay connected and keep their social networks humming.

Does genuine mental telepathy exist? Science has yet to prove that it does. Nevertheless, a visit to the New Age section of your bookstore will give you plenty to think about, including how big an industry ESP is.

Q Why does time seem to move faster as you get older?

A Many of the "benefits" of growing old seem to involve decreased speed. It takes longer to walk across the room because we're not as fleet of foot. We speak more slowly as our aged brains struggle to keep pace with our mouths. Amorous advances require a little more patience because of certain physiological transformations. And then there's the driving-slow-in-the-left-lane deal.

But nature appears to quicken one thing as we age: the passage of time. The older we get, the more often we find ourselves saying, "Really? That happened twelve years ago? I thought it was more like three years ago."

In 1975, University of Cincinnati professor Robert Lemlich published a paper on time perception. (We could swear it was more like 1988.) Working on the assumption that as a person ages, each year accounts for a smaller fraction of his or her entire life, Lemlich devised an equation comparing one year in the life of a forty-year-old to one year in the life of a ten-year-old. He concluded that time goes by twice as fast for the forty-year-old. To arrive at this finding, he divided ten years into forty, took the square root of that result, and ended up with the number two.

Understand? We don't, either. We just thought it necessary to include some science in the answer. But it's Lemlich's basic premise that's important: The longer you live, the shorter any given increment of time seems relative to the length of your life. Time isn't moving faster, but your perception of time changes.

Proof? When you're five, a year of kindergarten seems like an eternity. But when you're fifty, that annual prostate exam seems to come up about every six weeks.

Q Do blind people see in their dreams?

A This question presents a thorny conceptual problem. How do you measure what blind people imagine while they're asleep? What sort of technology exists that could allow one to peer into the unconscious minds of patients and see their innermost thoughts? Oh, wait—you could just ask them.

A number of studies have been conducted over the past half-century or so in which blind patients were asked to record the content of their dreams or discuss them during interviews. Each team of researchers arrived at the same conclusion: If the patients were congenitally blind (blind from birth) or lost their sight before the age of five, they had no visual content in their dreams (or waking imagination, for that matter). And although some congenitally blind participants reported visual aspects to their dreams, it was soon revealed that they weren't actually seeing. One eighteen-year-old subject described a dream in which she encountered a table adorned with two silver candelabras, but when asked how she knew which metal the candelabras were made from, she responded that they were "very smooth to touch." This is a sort of simulated sight, courtesy of the body's other senses.

Some researchers have used EEG readings (tests that monitor the electrical impulses in the brain) to try to uncover whether the congenitally blind or those who lost their sight before the age of five can see in their dreams. Tests of these blind people while they were dreaming recorded significant stimulation of the visual cortex, which is where the brain processes visual information received from the eyes. In one study, participants were able to draw pictures of their dreams upon waking.

Does this mean the blind were seeing? Not exactly. The visual cortex is also involved in processing auditory or tactile signals, especially in the blind, whose other senses endeavor to compensate for the lack of sight. Therefore, the ability of the blind to draw pictures of their dreams isn't surprising—it's not as if the blind have no conception of the world around them. For example, auditory cues, such as echoes, can be used to gauge the size of a room and an individual's position inside of it. If a blind person were to draw a picture of a dream that involved having a conversation inside a room, it stands to reason that the dreamer would be able to create a reasonable visual facsimile of that room. You probably wouldn't want to hang the picture on your wall, but chances are that you'd recognize what was being depicted.

This, however, doesn't equate to being able to really see in a dream. Consider it a mirage.

Q Are women more emotional than men?

A Get out your handkerchiefs, ladies. It's time for a chick flick, and we all know how emotional women get, don't we? Or do we? Are men really from Mars and women from Venus?

According to psychologist Ann Kring of Vanderbilt University, men react just as strongly to a sentimental flick as women do. In 1998, she asked male and female volunteers to watch the same movie with electrodes attached to their non-dominant palms in order to measure sweating and an increase in body temperature. The men got damp palms, just like the women. What they didn't get, however, were damp eyes. Women, Kring noted, were more likely to show their emotions through facial expressions and tears.

This finding meshes with the observations of Dr. William Frey II, author of *Crying: The Mystery of Tears*. After age eighteen, Frey contends, women cry four times as often as men. This may be due to the surge of prolactin—a hormone that triggers lactation after childbirth—in women's bodies as they reach adulthood. Prolactin is found throughout the female body—in blood, sweat, and, yes, tears.

How can men and women feel the same but behave so differently? University of California–Irvine researchers Larry Cahill and Lisa Kilpatrick made some startling discoveries in 2006 when they studied the amygdalas of thirty-six male and thirty-six female volunteers via brain scans. The amygdala is a small cluster of neurons in the brain that processes strong emotions, such as fear and aggression.

In men, the right side of the amygdala is most active; the neurons there connect with areas of the brain that govern physical movement, vision, and other outward-oriented functions. Women, in contrast, use the left side of the amygdala, which is connected to areas of the brain that monitor heart rate, blood pressure, and hormone levels.

How did these differences evolve? Cahill and Kilpatrick speculate that because women become pregnant, it might be more important for them to control what goes on inside their bodies rather than outside.

Just how significant are these differences in the context of everyday life? Linguist Deborah Tannen has spent nearly three decades analyzing how men and women speak. Armed with a tape recorder, she's eavesdropped on hundreds of conversations. In her bestselling book *You Just Don't Understand,* Tannen concludes that women use language to convey feelings while men use it to exchange information. These are broad generalizations, but her advice is valid: The keys to overcoming differences, she says, are patience, persistence, and compassion.

So walk a few blocks in your partner's shoes, be they stilettos or size-sixteen desert boots. And when you get to the movies, enjoy that sci-fi feature, the one about the Martian boy who meets the Venusian girl, and, well, you know the rest.

Q Does a baby feel the umbilical cord being cut off?

A Childbirth is one of life's greatest miracles—actually, it's a series of small miracles within that great miracle. Among them is the umbilical cord. A narrow tube of tissue that connects the fetus' navel with the placenta, the umbilical cord contains two umbilical arteries and one umbilical vein. The fetus' heart pumps blood to and from the placenta via the umbilical cord, drawing in nutrients and oxygen while sending away waste materials.

Once the baby is born, the umbilical cord is rendered unnecessary and needs to be cut. This is where the whole childbirth thing would logically take a sharp turn for the worse, but it doesn't.

And for that, we can thank one of those small miracles: Wharton's jelly.

No, we're not talking about a breakfast spread that's handcrafted in a New England village. Wharton's jelly is the soft connective tissue in the umbilical cord. A key feature of Wharton's jelly is its lack of nerve endings—this means that when the umbilical cord is clamped and cut, neither the mother nor the baby feels a thing. The joyful moment can continue, unsullied.

Q Could humans one day live to be 140?

A Yes, and it isn't a far-off possibility. Some scientists believe that within fifty years, people in industrialized nations will routinely live one hundred years or longer. When that time comes, you can bet that a few healthy, energetic individuals will be pushing 140, 145, 150, and beyond.

The average American these days is expected to live seventy-eight years, and the average life expectancy worldwide has been increasing by about two years every decade since the 1840s. Back then, Sweden boasted the population with the most impressive longevity: Healthy folks lived to the ripe old age of forty-five.

The increasing life expectancy is attributed to a number of factors, such as vaccinations, antibiotics, improved sanitation, and stricter food regulations. Furthermore, improved safety regulations in the workplace and on the road have helped to prevent fatal injuries.

Experts such as James Vaupel, director of the laboratory of survival and longevity at the Max Planck Institute in Germany, believe that life expectancy will continue to climb as techniques improve for preventing, diagnosing, and treating age-related maladies such as heart disease and cancer.

Centennial birthday parties should be commonplace by early in the twenty-second century. That may seem like a long way off, but consider that those centigenarians are being born now. The baby that your sister-in-law just brought home from the hospital may come close to reaching 140.

Without a crystal ball to forecast the medical advances we may achieve, it's impossible to say how long people eventually will be living. But as Daniel Perry, executive director of the Alliance for Aging Research, said, "There is no obvious barrier to living well beyond one hundred."

Q Is it possible to have a photographic memory?

A To correctly answer this question, we must carefully define the term "photographic memory." For example, your nitwit college friend who can recite thirty minutes of dialog from *Animal House* doesn't qualify. If this guy's memory is truly photographic, why was he on academic probation for four consecutive years?

No, the answer hinges on more than just having a very good memory. Consider Akira Haraguchi, who memorized Pi to the

83,431st decimal and recited each one over the course of thirteen straight hours in 2006, then followed up with a recitation to the 100,000th in sixteen-plus hours. Although this certainly sounds like a photographic memory, Haraguchi admitted to using a complex mnemonic system in which he substituted the numbers with letters to help him remember the colossal string of digits.

Simply retaining information through repetition doesn't qualify as a photographic memory. If that were the case, almost everyone would have one. Put another way, wouldn't you be concerned for your dopey friend if after viewing *Animal House* two dozen times, he *couldn't* reel off a half hour of John Belushi quotes?

Defining a photographic memory as a person's ability to recall everything he or she has ever seen or heard isn't valid, either. No human being on record has demonstrated such an ability.

However, there is a middle ground between learning though repetition and natural, machine-like retention. Eidetic memory is a phenomenon similar to the popular conception of a photographic memory, and it has been well documented in the medical community.

Individuals with an eidetic memory are literally able to retain a snapshot of images they've viewed, much like a camera does. For example, scientists who are attempting to diagnose an eidetic memory often show a patient a picture—sometimes for as little as thirty seconds—and then ask very specific questions about details of the picture.

While people with eidetic memories are able to recall such details quite accurately, discrepancies often creep in, and their retention rarely lasts more than a few minutes. Furthermore, this ability occurs predominantly in children, and preadolescents displaying this talent almost always lose it when they reach adulthood. Scientists can't fully explain why children develop and then lose an eidetic memory; the theory is that verbal thinking eventually replaces a visually oriented system.

Eidetic memories are no doubt impressive to behold, but they're really not what we're looking for in our search for a photographic memory, are they? Thus, it is our duty to confirm that the world is a slightly less magical place than you might want to believe it is. Photographic memory does not exist, and your college buddy really is unexceptional in every way.

Q Are fat people more jolly?

A "Personal size and mental sorrow have certainly no necessary proportions," wrote eighteenth- and nineteenth-century novelist Jane Austen, the exquisitely perspicacious observer of human nature. "A large bulky figure has as good a right to be in deep affliction, as the most graceful set of limbs in the world. But, fair or not fair, there are unbecoming conjunctions, which reason will patronize in vain—which taste cannot tolerate—which ridicule will seize."

In other words, long before Weight Watchers, Anglo-European society had stereotyped fat people as cheerful and jolly and skinny folks as sensitive and poetic. In Austen's world, a pensive, plump person appeared faintly ridiculous to the public eye.

Not that thin people were necessarily admired. Around 1600, Shakespeare's Julius Caesar declared, "Let me have men about me that are fat.... Yond Cassius has a lean and hungry look; He thinks too much: such men are dangerous."

Is there any scientific basis for the assumption that thin equals crafty and fat equals affable? Psychologist William Sheldon thought so. In the mid-twentieth century, he pioneered the idea of the somatotype, or body type, to explain personality traits.

According to Sheldon, people could be divided into three groups: endomorphs, mesomorphs, and ectomorphs. Endomorphs were round, soft, easygoing, and relaxed; mesomorphs were muscular, aggressive, and adventurous; and ectomorphs were thin, high-strung, and quick-witted. On the down side, endomorphs could be lazy; mesomorphs could be power-grabbing thugs; and ectomorphs could be lean, hungry, and dangerous.

Sheldon's body types gave generations of pop psychologists a lot to chew on. Unfortunately, he was never quite clear about his research methods, which seem to have consisted mostly of taking pictures of naked college students—the so-called "posture photos" that were an embarrassing ritual for Ivy League freshmen for nearly thirty years, from the 1940s through the 1960s.

Nevertheless, the question remains: Is there any correlation between weight and personality? These days, researchers are more likely to find depressed heavy people and cheerful thin ones. A study sponsored by the National Institute of Mental Health in 2006 showed that, compared to people of normal weight, the obese were 25 percent more likely to suffer from mood or anxiety disorders. Given society's negative attitudes toward excess weight, it's not hard to understand why fat people would be depressed.

However, another study at the University of California–San Francisco, indicated that stress might be a major factor in overeating, raising the prospect that depression might be a cause of obesity rather than a result. And still other studies show that the relationship between body size and self-esteem is not so easy to pin down—kind of what Jane Austen herself might have said.

Q How smart do you have to be to be considered a genius?

A We all know a moron when we see one, but geniuses can be a bit harder to pick out of a lineup.

The simplest gauge of mental capacity is intelligence quotient, or IQ. Different IQ tests use different types of questions, but they all share a basic scoring system called the Binet Scale (after French psychologist Alfred Binet, who came up with it in the early nineteen hundreds).

In the modern version of the Binet Scale, 100 is the median score, and "average intelligence" is any score between 90 and 109. Scores of 110 or higher indicate superior intelligence, and scores of 140 or higher mean truly exceptional intelligence—less than 1 percent of the population is in this rarefied category.

In the early twentieth century, researchers who studied intelligence in children began setting a genius benchmark, typically between 130 and 140. They assumed that with this kind of brainpower, these child geniuses would be smart enough to succeed at just about any mental task. The definition caught on with parents and psychologists, and 140 became the most common magic number. So if you crack this barrier, you have a defendable rationale for sporting that "Genius at Work" T-shirt.

But let's not get ahead of ourselves—today, many psychologists believe that IQ in itself is an incomplete, and perhaps even a flawed, measure of intelligence. This is partly because of a concept that was first advanced in 1983, when psychologist Howard Gardner rocked the profession with his theory of multiple intelligences. Gardner posited that people exhibit seven separate types of intelligence: linguistic, logical-mathematical, spatial, musical, bodily-kinesthetic, interpersonal, and intrapersonal. Conventional IQ tests are focused on linguistic and logical-mathematical intelligence. They are, then, a bad measure of other types of intelligence; for example, an IQ test won't reveal artistic or athletic genius.

Another problem with IQ tests, at least where we geniuses are concerned, is that the questions don't measure innovation—the ability to make completely original connections, or what might be called "flashes of genius." Many people with very high IQs end up doing nothing remarkable their whole lives. Does it make sense to call them geniuses, just because they can answer test questions that have established, known answers? As smart as

Einstein was, he never would have gone down in history as a genius if he hadn't come up with new ideas.

A more useful, but much more subjective, definition of "genius" is a person with exceptional intelligence (of any sort) that enables him or her to make creative leaps that change how we see or interact with the world. It might be a new way of painting (Picasso's cubism), a new way of explaining natural phenomena (Newton's laws of motion), or an amazing invention (Ron Popeil's Veg-O-Matic).

So, Mr. Smarty Pants, even if you do have a sky-high IQ, don't rest on your laurels. We want to see some brilliant ideas out of you—otherwise, we're taking the T-shirt away.

Q Who decided suntans are attractive?

A Suntans have been in and out of fashion throughout history. In many primitive societies, the sun was revered as the center of the spiritual universe, and a perpetual tan was a sign of religious fidelity. In our own slightly less primitive time, sun worship is still common, but the purpose is anything but religious. We do it because, as noted spray-on tan enthusiast Paris Hilton would put it, "that's hot."

How did it get that way? In the nineteenth century, debutantes and socialites—the Paris Hiltons of their day—would have been praised for their paleness. To compare a lady's skin to alabaster—a hard, white mineral used in sculpture—was to offer a high compliment indeed. But toward the end of the nineteenth century, doctors began to realize that sunlight is necessary for good health, as it promotes vitamin formation in the body. This didn't make suntans attractive overnight, but it helped dissolve the stigma against them. In the twentieth century, tans grew more and more popular from aesthetic and social perspectives, even as evidence mounted that linked sun exposure to skin cancer.

If one person deserves credit for really sparking the current suntan rage, it's famed fashion designer Coco Chanel. She was sunburned while on vacation one summer in the 1920s, and her resulting tan became all the rage. "The 1929 girl must be tanned," she would later say. "A golden tan is the index of chic." A pronouncement of this kind of out-and-out shallowness is perfectly suited for today's world, too, though it might translate to the current youth vernacular as something more like, "OMG tans rule!!!!" It's clear that Coco was on to something: As a society, we do think that tans are attractive.

Experts say that a suntan nowadays suggests someone who is rugged, athletic, and unafraid of things. It also suggests wealth, leisure, and the freedom to be outside while others are slaving away indoors. This represents a dramatic change from the nineteenth century, when tanned skin was more likely to indicate a life of manual labor in the fields—a sign of someone at the bottom of the social ladder rather than the top.

That's the sociological explanation. There's also an explanation that centers on evolutionary psychology—this theory has to do with the "attractiveness of averageness." Studies have shown that when there is a heterogeneity (or range) of genes present in a person, the resulting face is more average—it is free of unusual

236 · Why Won't Men Ask for Directions?

quirks of size or shape. Over the millennia, humans have come to innately understand that such a person is also more robust physically, without the genetic weaknesses or flaws inherent in inbreeding.

When a fair-skinned person's face is tan, it appears to be closer to the overall human average, theoretical as this might be. If it seems far-fetched, consider something: Studies have shown that people of all skin colors tend to believe that the most attractive faces have hues that are between light and dark. In other words, the folks we find most alluring have suntans.

Q What causes stuttering?

A This one stumps the scientists, although they're not quite as stumped as they once were. Stuttering takes four major forms: repeating consonant sounds, repeating entire syllables, extending vowel sounds, and involuntarily stopping between sounds. It typically begins between ages two and five, when we're rapidly developing our language abilities; tripping up on words at this time is a normal part of learning to talk.

In the 1950s and 1960s, the leading theory was that overbearing parenting caused stuttering. This explanation held that a parent who overreacted to a young child's normal hesitation or repetition (by scolding or panicking, say) caused the kid to develop a fear of stuttering. This anxiety was thought to lead to stuttering in later years. In other words, you become a stutterer because you think you're a stutterer.

Today's leading theory points to biological factors—not environmental factors—as the causes of the most common form of the affliction, developmental stuttering. Developmental stuttering appears to be genetic: It pops up in families across many generations, and there is a significantly higher concordance of stuttering among identical twins than among other siblings.

Another type of stuttering is neurogenic stuttering, which can occur after a stroke or after a head trauma or other type of brain injury. The least common type is acquired stuttering, which can be evident both in children and adults who have suffered emotional trauma.

While brain imaging doesn't show structural abnormalities in stutterers, it does reveal odd activity patterns in parts of the brain that involve speech. Brain imaging on adult stutterers has revealed increased activity in the areas of the brain that control speech motor control; this might overactivate the muscles involved in speaking, which could then cause stutterers to freeze up when words are being vocalized.

At the same time, imaging has shown the auditory processing area of a stutterer's brain to be less active than normal. It's not clear whether these abnormal patterns are causes or symptoms of stuttering. In some cases, however, using electronic devices that alter how stutterers hear their voices has resulted in great improvement in speech.

Although most experts agree that stuttering has biological roots, there's strong evidence that environmental factors can exacerbate it. Many experts believe that the more anxious someone is about stuttering, the harder the problem is to overcome. Speech pathologists recommend that parents don't hurry a stuttering child or do anything to make the youngster more self-conscious. Some stutterers have benefited from a change in environment; screen star Bruce Willis, for example, found relief from stuttering through acting.

No surefire cure has been found, but speech therapy seems to greatly reduce the severity of stuttering. At least scientists aren't laying guilt trips on parents anymore.

Q Why aren't people covered in hair like other primates?

A Life would be much more confusing at the zoo, for one thing. Cover us in fur and the line between ape and man gets a lot blurrier.

Scientists have proposed a few explanations for why people are mostly hairless. In the 1970s, the hot theory was that early humans entered a semi-aquatic phase—they spent their days catching fish and eating plant life in shallow waters. Like whales and hippos, humans lost their fur in favor of a layer of fat under the skin, which is a better insulator in the water.

But there are some holes in this theory—the most notable being that hanging out in African lakes and rivers is dangerous, thanks to crocodiles and nasty water-born parasites. If we had spent that much time in the water, critics say, we would have developed better defenses against the parasitic worms and such that still kill people in Africa today.

Speaking of parasites, a more recent theory speculates that we lost our fur as a defense against lice, fleas, and the like. When you're covered in fur, parasites are a major problem—but the insulating benefits of a flea-ridden coat of fur make the problem worth enduring. Until you've invented clothing, that is. As soon as humans could make their own clothes and build their own shelters, fur became a liability.

The problem with this theory is that the timing doesn't work—scientists have traced our fur loss back about 1.7 million years, yet evidence of clothing goes back only about forty thousand years. Still, even if parasite-avoidance wasn't the driving force in our loss of fur, it might help to explain why we think smooth, hairless skin is sexy today. Think back to our caveman days, and you'll see why we might have been hardwired to favor hairless-ness. If you had no body hair, a potential mate could clearly see whether you had parasites; if you didn't, it suggested that you were healthy and would produce strong offspring.

But back to how we lost our fur in the first place. The most popu-lar theory nowadays is that the scorching savannah was just too darn hot. As humans gradually developed a new foraging and hunting lifestyle, they began leaving the cool jungles behind for long treks in the hot sun.

And then, just as now, humans cooled off by sweating. As our hirsute ancestors chased their prey across the vast savannahs, they would have soaked their furry coats in no time, making it even more likely that their bodies would overheat. Having no fur enables sweat to cool the skin—and, thus, the body—directly and effectively. In our ancestors' new broiling environment, the benefits of keeping cool in the daytime would have outweighed the problem of poor insulation at night. Meanwhile, our primate cousins never left the cool jungles, so they never made the shift to hairlessness.

Humans retained the hair on their heads, it seems, because these locks help to keep the brain cool—when the sun beats down on our heads, it heats up the outermost layer of hair rather than fry the scalp directly. As for the stuff on our armpits and around our groins, the leading theory is that this hair accentuates phero- mones (chemicals that are supposed to entice the opposite sex through the sense of smell). Who knew that B.O. is sexier than perfume and cologne?

Chapter Thirteen

MORE GOOD STUFF

Q What happened to all the gravy trains?

A Vegetarians are so smug, running around with their "ethics" and "environment" and "health." Blah, blah, blah. Listen up, plant gobblers: You can have your rabbit food. Why? We've got a little something called gravy.

That's right—gravy, the Nectar of the Carnivorous Gods. Made from the juices of slowly cooking meat, gravy is a square meal in itself. Too bad you can't have it. Even worse, when the gravy train finally arrives to take we meat eaters to the Promised Land of milk and gravy, you'll be left behind to wander the planet aimlessly.

Okay, as it turns out, the Bible doesn't actually say a single thing about gravy trains transporting meat eaters to paradise during the apocalypse. More alarming, it appears as if there were never any trains that carried gravy. Where, then, did this curious little phrase come from?

Gravy has long been a symbol of luxury and privilege. For many centuries, meat was prohibitively expensive, and gravy—which, as we said, is made from the juices of animals that are being cooked—was a real delicacy. This thick, delicious sauce has been around since at least medieval times, and it's probably not surprising that it first appears in a recipe book that was used by King Richard II's chefs. Gravy was part of such timeless recipes as "connynges in grauey." (What? You've never chowed down on delicious connynges?)

By the nineteenth century, the word "gravy" was being used to refer to anything of profit or benefit, especially if it could be obtained with little work. But where the "train" came in is a mystery. Some etymologists suggest that it referenced easy money for little work on certain train routes in the late nineteenth century; another explanation is that it might have arisen among the train-riding hobo communities. Or the phrase might simply have developed in popular lingo as a clever way to describe living the good life.

So even though we meat eaters are going to have to find a different way to get to the Promised Land, a gravy train is still a pretty awesome thing.

Q When did it become socially acceptable to go out without a hat?

A   Take a gander at some photos from when your grandparents were young. Just a few generations ago, in any outdoor public space—whether it was the bleachers at a baseball game or the sidewalks of a city street—the chances were good that almost everybody was wearing a hat. Depending on the year and the season, the type varied—for men, it could've been a fedora, a porkpie, a straw boater, or a derby; for women, the styles were endlessly diverse—but a hat was clearly a necessary accessory.

Sometime during the middle years of the twentieth century that changed, and hats dropped out of the daily wardrobe. Exactly when and why this happened is a matter of some speculation. One popularly held belief is that President John F. Kennedy killed the hat when he chose not to wear one to his inauguration in 1961. The problem with this theory is that Kennedy *did* wear a hat to his inauguration—not just any hat, but a silk top hat. True, he didn't wear it while taking the oath of office or while delivering his inaugural address, but you have to go back to Woodrow Wilson's second inauguration in 1917 to find a president who donned headgear during his address.

As author and newspaper columnist Neil Steinberg observes in his book *Hatless Jack: The President, the Fedora, and the History of an American Style,* the struggling U.S. hat-making industry did make overtures to JFK to try to get him to wear hats in public more often than he did, hoping to capitalize on the handsome president's potential to sway tastes in fashion. But by that time, the handwriting was on the wall, and the hatters knew it. Hats had been on their way out for decades.

Steinberg pinpoints the 1890s as the beginning of the end for hats, and he says that newspaper reports from the era indicate that it was younger women who led the charge. Women had begun removing their hats in theaters as courtesies to the people seated behind them, and soon hatless women were common in all sorts of public places. Before long, men followed suit.

There were complaints, of course. But the fact that hatlessness had become a matter of public debate is a solid sign that the new look had also become widespread. It took a few generations for the hat to fall out of favor altogether; by the 1970s, hat-wearing was generally associated with old farts who were cling-ing to fashions from the past.

Q Which one is spotted most frequently: the Loch Ness Monster, Bigfoot, or Elvis?

A The skeptical answer is easy: It's a three-way tie, with each nonexistent creature being spotted zero times. But what fun is that?

Just for the sake of argument, let's say that each of these paranormal freaks—the slimy eel cruising the depths of the loch in Scotland, the hairy ape roaming the woods of the Pacific Northwest, and the hunka hunka burnin' love haunting the fast-food drive-thrus of the South—does, in fact, exist. Which one makes the most public appearances?

The Loch Ness Monster definitely has time on its side. Sightings date back to the sixth century, when the beast allegedly attacked a monk named Columba who was trying to rescue a swimmer. (After his death, Columba became a saint, for reasons having nothing to do with his Nessie wrestling.) But appearances of the monster were infrequent until the twentieth century, when Nessie turned into something of a publicity hound. It started in 1934 when the London *Daily Mail* published a grainy photograph that purported to show the creature's head rising above the surface of the water. Ever since that first taste of mass media fame, the monster has been making fairly regular appearances, if we can believe the reports.

Bigfoot—or Sasquatch, to his friends—also has a long history under his belt. Even before the arrival of Europeans, he was glimpsed in the towering forests of the northwest, in what is now northern California, Oregon, Washington, and British Columbia. A seemingly nonviolent bipedal fellow covered in thick fur, Bigfoot generally shows up in the woods and then skulks off once he realizes that he's been spotted. The Bigfoot phenomenon really took off in 1958, when giant footprints were found in a logging camp in Humboldt County, California. This seminal event in Bigfoot history was later tainted when the family of Ray Wallace, a logger who worked in that camp, revealed that Wallace had staged the whole thing. Nevertheless, this hoax didn't end Bigfoot mania—the legend lives on.

Elvis Presley, meanwhile, is a slightly less mythical creature than Bigfoot or Nessie. Evidence suggests that a man of that name did indeed walk the earth, consuming large quantities of fried peanut butter and banana sandwiches while producing a long series of hit songs and terrible movies. Since the reports of his death in 1977, Elvis has continued to live in the not-so-suspicious minds of many of his devoted followers. From Kalamazoo to Kansas City, astonished correspondents have told stories of seeing the King of Rock 'n' Roll pumping gas, buying groceries, or delivering pizzas.

A psychiatrist, Dr. Donald Hinton, said that he had secretly prescribed pain killers for Elvis during the 1990s; later, Hinton published a book that he claimed to have co-written with a man named "Jesse," whom he said was Elvis incognito. There's a reason you've never heard of this book, and it has nothing to do with any of the vast cover-up conspiracies.

And that's the problem with determining which one of these guys has the highest profile: Among the reports from the poor souls who honestly believe they've had encounters with them, you also find plenty of obvious fakes and pranks, arranged by people who are looking for publicity, money, or just a good laugh. It's impossible to tally the number of—for lack of a better word—"legitimate" sightings.

But we at F.Y.I. headquarters aren't afraid of a challenge, no matter how preposterous it is. We thought long and hard about this one and argued endlessly amongst ourselves in order to reach a consensus. So, our pick for the winner? Until either Nessie or 'Foot plays a string of sold-out concerts in Las Vegas, we're backing the King.

Q Has anyone gotten rich off chain letters?

A If people have, they haven't come forward publicly. And well they shouldn't, since the only way to get rich from chain letters is to perpetrate a devious scam.

Chain letters go back to the nineteenth century, and there have been many versions over the years. The "get rich quick" variety typically goes something like this: You receive a letter with the names and addresses of ten strangers. You send a dollar to each person on the list, then write a new version of the letter, removing the person at the top of the list and adding your name and address to the bottom of the list. You send copies to ten other people. Those ten people recruit ten other people, who recruit ten other people, and so on. Seven cycles after you send your letters, ten million people each will send you a dollar. And just like that—you're rich!

But it doesn't really work out that way. Any money-making chain letter is doomed to fail because the response rate will be abysmal. Nobody tracks these response rates, but for comparison, consider response rates for professional direct-mail campaigns that use expensive mailing lists of qualified buyers. The median order-generation response rate for these campaigns is around 1 percent. In other words, approximately one out of every hundred recipients of a professional mailing will spend money in response to an ad.

It's highly unlikely that chain letters that are sent randomly will reach even that modest level of success. If you did receive a dollar from a hundred letters that you sent, you paid forty-four dollars in postage, so you are down forty-three dollars. Even if you did pique the interest of a fellow get-rich-quick believer, what's to stop him or her from sending on the letter without enclosing any money?

Scam artists are the ones who are most likely to haul in the money from chain letters. One common ploy is to charge a fee for helping someone launch a chain letter. A scam artist might charge a hundred dollars for a list of "leads"—i.e., the names and addresses of people who supposedly are likely to respond to chain letters. A scam artist typically uses a post office box as a mailing address, which makes it difficult for victims to track him or her down.

Participating in a chain letter that involves soliciting money is illegal, per the United States Postal Code, which prohibits running lotteries through the mail. Chain letters are considered illegal gambling, since a person is paying for the chance to win money. The law doesn't apply to chain letters that don't involve money (the "forward this on for good luck" variety). Those are legal, no matter how incredibly annoying they might be.

Q Can we really expect good advice if it's only worth two cents?

A You get, the saying goes, what you pay for. It's true with wine, it's true with prostitutes, and it's definitely true with advice. Only the desperate and the gullible would take free advice from old-lady newspaper columnists or hosts of radio call-in shows. If you need real advice, find someone who charges for it. But it's probably best to make sure that they charge more than two cents. Come to think of it, where did the convention of two-cent advice come from? It's doubtful that psychiatrists were ever that cheap.

As you no doubt know by now, we here at F.Y.I. headquarters can't resist proffering our opinion at the slightest provocation, so here are our two cents on the subject. (Bet you saw *that* coming.) There are several theories regarding the origin of the phrase "throwing in one's two cents."

One holds that this expression dates back to the mid- or late nineteenth century in the United States. Two cents as a slang expression may be related to the fact that something very cheap back then cost two cents (sort of like how we now use the expressions "three-dollar haircut" and "three-dollar steak").

However, some people suggest that the phrase is actually older than that. According to these folks, "two cents' worth" is a transatlantic translation of the British word "twopenny," "tuppence," or "two-penneth."

Yet another group suggests that two cents derives from the "two bits" that were the standard ante for a poker match—the two cents, then, would be the fee to enter the discussion. While this is intriguing to consider, there is no documentary evidence to back it up.

So there you have it—we've provided proof positive that advice worth two cents isn't advice worth taking. And you spent a heck of a lot more than two cents on this book, so you know that you can trust us.

Q Are there real ghostbusters?

A Your house is oozing with ectoplasm. Strange moaning and wailing keep you up at night. Who you gonna call? If you're a fan of old movies, you know the answer: Ghostbusters.

Or you could try Bonnie Vent, the founder of the San Diego Paranormal Research Project—though she's really more of a ghost whisperer than a ghostbuster. In fact, Vent prefers the term "spirit advocate." According to a 2008 article in the *New York Times,* she can cleanse your home of spooky visitors with a little friendly coaxing.

Vent doesn't believe in rituals—instead, she engages the ghost in conversation to find out why it's there. "Spirit people are people," she says. "You have to get to the root cause." Vent's spirit advocacy is not cheap: She charges $125 an hour for her services. And sometimes the ghost decides to stick around anyway, in which case she recommends that you "try to work out a livable situation." Conveniently, Vent doubles as a real estate agent and invites potential buyers and sellers of haunted houses to advertise on her Web site.

If your definition of a "livable situation" includes only the living, call Fiona Broome, who bills herself as a "paranormal investigator." Broome, like Vent, recommends talking to the ghost. If that doesn't work, she resorts to an arsenal of traditional remedies, including garlic, sea salt, holy water, and hex signs. Or she offers this tip: Place your shoes at the foot of the bed pointed in opposite directions. This apparently causes the ghost to become so confused that it will depart to seek more orderly digs.

Mary Ann Winkowski, another buster of ghosts, suggests burning bundles of white sage, known as smudge sticks, to banish ghosts from the premises. Smudge sticks are used in many Native American cleansing ceremonies, and Winkowski claims that they have helped her to rout ghosts from homes, offices, schools, and even cars. Winkowski serves as a consultant for the popular CBS television drama *Ghost Whisperer*, as does her fellow psychic, James Van Praagh.

Van Praagh describes himself as a "clairesentient"—that is, one who is able to receive information from spirits through his emotions. Unlike other ghost whisperers, Van Praagh doesn't seek to get rid of ghosts. Rather, he specializes in locating spirits for those who want to connect with dead loved ones.

Patty A. Wilson of the Ghost Research Foundation spends more time looking for ghosts than getting rid of them. The author of a series of books on ghost hunting in Pennsylvania, she acknowledges that "ghosts stories are not neat and clean. They're real stories about real people." And they don't always end with the ghost drifting off into the great beyond.

Q Do coffins come with lifetime guarantees?

A How long does a coffin last? Some, like the sarcophagi of the ancient Egyptians, can hold up for centuries. Others, like the Ecopod, a coffin made of recycled newspapers by a British company of the same name, are intended to biodegrade within a few years.

Has any coffin maker offered a lifetime guarantee? Tough question—the best we could find are rumors. People in Indiana have claimed that the state's Batesville Casket Company used to sell caskets with lifetime guarantees, but the company wouldn't confirm this assertion.

Like many casket manufacturers, the Batesville company produces waterproof caskets that are guaranteed not to leak for between twenty and seventy-five years, depending on the price of the casket. Perhaps at one time an overeager funeral director assured grieving families that the deluxe seventy-five-year, leak-proof model would keep their dearly departed safe for at least a lifetime, "guaranteed."

When arranging a funeral, it helps to remember that only the coffin can be guaranteed to last, not the body inside. In fact, the more airtight the coffin, the more rapidly a corpse will disintegrate due to the activity of anaerobic microbes. These bacteria, which thrive in the absence of oxygen, can literally liquefy a dead body. With a little fresh air, a body will decay more slowly. But fast or slow, nature decrees that all bodies inevitably decay, no matter how fancy the coffin.

Q Why aren't green cards green?

A Immigration has been a point of confusion and contention in the United States for years. And it shows no signs of letting up, with guest-worker programs being debated in Congress, self-labeled "Minutemen" patrolling the border with

Mexico, and fantastic scenarios involving infrared cameras and electronic devices tracking illegal immigrants. Of course, the problem may be even more fundamental. Has anybody in Congress noticed that green cards aren't even green?

The so-called green card—technically known as a Permanent Resident Card, or Form I-551—actually changes colors periodically to stymie counterfeiters. These cards are given to immigrants to identify them as lawful, permanent resident aliens of the United States. There are a number of ways in which immigrants can get green cards, including marriage to a U.S. citizen, certain types of employment by an American company, and through a "green card lottery" operated by the United States Citizenship and Immigration Service (the unwieldy new name for the old Immigration and Naturalization Service, or INS).

For a long time, green cards didn't exist at all. Instead, immigrants who registered with the government were issued receipts as proof of registration. Unfortunately, there was no real way to tell whether an immigrant in possession of a receipt was a temporary visitor or a permanent resident. It wasn't until after World War II that the government began issuing different forms of identification based on the type of immigrant one was. The early cards (issued before 1976) that were given to permanent residents were green in color, giving rise to the term "green card." Over the years, the design and color of the Permanent Resident Card has changed many times, but "green card" has remained in the lexicon.

Despite its illogic, the term is in such common use that it probably isn't going anywhere. Nevertheless, as the U.S. immigration policy leans further and further toward the xenophobic, it seems to be the perfect time for the green card to be updated with more appropriate nomenclature. Our suggestion? A "get out of jail free" card.

Q Does speed reading really work?

A You'll learn more through speed reading than by not reading at all, but that's about as far as we'll go. Evidence suggests that chugging through a book at your normal speed is the only way to fully comprehend it. (Sorry to burst the bubbles of any aspiring speed readers.)

The basic idea of speed reading is to recognize multiple words in a phrase at once rather than to read each word individually. This requires that you stop "subvocalizing" words—saying each word in your head. Speed readers typically use a finger as a pacer; they move it over the words on the page faster than the brain can pre-vocalize.

With enough practice, a person supposedly adapts to the pace and can understand the meaning of text without subvocalizing each word. According to its proponents, the technique can boost reading speed by a hundred to 350 words per minute, to more than seven hundred words per minute; best of all, a person still comprehends the material being scanned.

Scientific research says otherwise. In a 1987 study, psychologists at Carnegie Mellon University compared reading comprehension among 240-words-per-minute readers, trained speed readers, and untrained skimmers (readers who skip words to get the gist of the text). The study used an easy text sample (a *Reader's Digest* article) and a difficult one (a *Scientific American* article). The speed readers and skimmers did nearly as well as the normal readers in answering questions related to the general subject but significantly worse when asked about specific details. Other studies have yielded similar results.

Of course, speed reading still can be useful—even if it's only a honed form of skimming text, it's a valuable skill. Just don't expect miracles. If you want to boast to your friends that you've *truly* read *War and Peace,* you'll have to slog through it the hard way.

Q Where is the dirtiest place in the house?

A Believe it or not, there's a place in the house that's even dirtier than the toilet or the trash can. We're talking about the kitchen sink.

Say what? How can the place where you wash things get so scuzzy? Well, most people use the kitchen sink to rinse and prepare items like chicken carcasses and store-bought fruits and vegetables.

According to Dr. Philip Tierno, director of New York University's microbiology department and the author of *The Secret Life of Germs,* these raw foods carry tons of potential pathogens, including salmonella, campylobacter, and *E. coli.* And you're just splish-splashing and spreading them around.

Right now, your kitchen sink's faucet handles and basin are probably teeming with microscopic creepy-crawlies. In fact, there are typically more than five hundred thousand bacteria per square inch in the sink drain alone! The average garbage bin has only about 411 bacteria per square inch. Grossed out yet? Well, there's more.

What about those damp dishrags and sponges that you toss into the sink? You know, the ones that you use to wipe down the kitchen counter? Tierno says that they can hold "literally billions of bacteria." Dr. Charles Gerba (a.k.a. Dr. Germ), an environmental microbiology professor at the University of Arizona, suggests that it might be better to live like a slobby bachelor than to meticulously clean kitchen surfaces with a salmonella-soaked sink sponge. According to Gerba's findings, your kitchen sink is dirtier than a post-flush toilet bowl. Go ahead, take a moment to gag.

Done gagging? Now, grab your scrub brush. You can have a much cleaner kitchen sink in a jiffy. Just mix one tablespoon of chlorine bleach with one quart of water, and use this solution to scrub your sink basin clean. Tierno recommends that you do this twice a week. In between, clean your kitchen sink and counter with an antibacterial product every time you prepare or rinse food.

As for sanitizing those cross-contaminated kitchen sponges, throw them in the washing machine with bleach, run them through the dishwasher's dryer cycle, or nuke them for one minute at high power in the microwave. Even then, don't use a sponge for more than a month. Or you can do away with kitchen sponges altogether. Wipe up food spills with paper towels and dump everything into the trash—where dirty stuff belongs.

Q What's so great about Swiss bank accounts?

A If all you want is free checking and access to a picked-over basket of lollipops, there's no reason to open a Swiss bank account. But if you happen to have a spare million lying around, it could be a top-shelf choice—especially if you want to keep your loot under wraps. Secrecy and stability are the main advantages of a Swiss bank account, and both of these qualities have deep roots in Switzerland's history.

Switzerland's main claim to fame—besides yodeling, chocolate, and holes in cheese—is its history of neutrality. For hundreds of years, the Swiss have taken great pains to steer clear of conflicts and restrictive treaties, fighting only when a nation threatens their borders. This national obsession with minding ones own business was shared by Swiss bankers, who developed a tradition of secrecy and extreme discretion.

The Swiss government codified this tradition in the Swiss Banking Act of 1934, which established strict rules for banking secrecy and fiscal responsibility. The act was largely a protective measure to prevent the Nazis from demanding funds from German citizens' Swiss accounts. The new law specified that sharing secret account information, even with the Swiss government, was a criminal act, punishable by a fine of fifty thousand Swiss francs or six months in jail.

This guaranteed privacy made Swiss bank accounts a handy repository for Americans who wanted to hide income from the Internal Revenue Service. Swiss banks wouldn't waive their depositors' privacy rights if the depositors were accused of tax evasion (in other words, failure to declare taxable income). The banks would share information with foreign governments only if the depositors' tax evasion rose to the level of documented fraud—if accounting records were falsified, for example.

But this legendary policy of privacy has been eroding. The United States and Switzerland signed an agreement in 2003 to share account information if either government had "a reasonable suspicion that the [depositors'] conduct would constitute tax fraud or the like." This significantly loosened the standard of evidence. In 2008, the Swiss bank UBS shared information on approximately seventy clients with the U.S. justice department as part of a tax evasion investigation. Swiss banks must also reveal account information related to certain civil cases, such as divorce and inheritance claims.

Even if Swiss banks are no longer the gold standard of discretion, secretive millionaires can still find plenty of tight-lipped bankers in notorious tax havens such as the Cayman Islands. But these banks can't match the Swiss record of financial stability. By avoiding military conflict, Switzerland has been immune to many of the troubles that have plagued other European nations' economies. The Swiss have also rigidly enforced conservative financial policies over the years. For example, Swiss law requires that at least 40 percent of the value of the Swiss franc is backed by gold reserves. And in the event of a bank failure, institutions that are members of the Swiss Bankers Association are required to quickly return all funds to their depositors.

While they're not quite as top-secret as spy thrillers suggest, the Swiss have some impressive banking chops. And they probably have good candy at the drive-thru windows, too.

Q How many kids have found razor blades in their candy apples?

A Halloween, All Hallows Eve, Samhain. Whatever you call it, October 31 is the night a kid's dreams come true. Not only do children get to dress up in costumes, but they also get to stand on their neighbors' porches and collect candy.

But it's not all fun and games. Parents are cautioned yearly to never allow their children to eat unwrapped candy that has been collected on Halloween night. Whenever a child gets sick around the end of October and there's even the slightest chance that the illness is related to eating tainted candy, alarmist news stations call for parents to dump everything their children brought home. While these reports might be broadcast with the best of intentions—ensuring the safety of our children—almost all of them wind up being false alarms.

Sociologists refer this as the "myth of the Halloween sadist." It's been causing yearly widespread panic since at least the 1970s, when a child died from an overdose of heroin that was said to have been given to him via Halloween candy. (This turned out to be untrue; the heroin belonged to an uncle, and it was hidden away in the kid's Halloween loot by family members in an attempt to keep the uncle out of jail.) Since then, similar incidents have occurred, and in nearly every case, Halloween candy hasn't turned out to be the offender.

There have been more cases of foreign objects in Halloween goods than of tainted candy. In the late 1960s, New Jersey saw a rash of apples that did indeed have razor blades inserted into them—enough to warrant state legislative action on the topic—

but few of the cases involved actual injury. The most notable case of tampering occurred in 2000, when a man put needles in Snickers bars and handed them out to neighborhood children. No one, however, was seriously hurt.

The myth of dangerous candy persists today partly due to young pranksters. By taking candy that has been collected (say, your little brother's stash) and inserting something mildly dangerous, the prankster spooks an entire neighborhood and gets a good laugh. Urban legend debunker and sociologist Joel Best reports one such case, in which a child approached his parents with a candy bar that was sprinkled with ant poison.

The child, it turned out, did the sprinkling. It was good for a quick laugh, maybe, but these kinds of pranks perpetuate the notion that Halloween is a night for real parental fear.

Q Why do old men wear their pants so high?

A Age is the great equalizer. No matter how hot you are when you're young, no matter how cool and stylish you manage to look through adulthood and into middle age, Father Time always has the last laugh. Our F.Y.I. medical staff refers to it as the Old Coot stage of life.

Among the afflictions that the male body must endure as it enters the Old Coot stage are two significant and merciless adjustments to the physique: (1) Fat gathers around the abdominal area while disappearing from other areas, and (2) muscle tone deteriorates. This translates to an expansion of the midsection and a simultaneous reduction in the hips and buttocks. In layman's terms, we call this a huge gut and no ass. And it all adds up to one cruel sartorial reality: Your body has lost its shape, so your pants just won't stay up.

Your pants need a waist and a butt to hang from. Once you lose those features, the only thing left to work with is that giant spare tire that you call a belly. So you've got to hike those pants up over the bulge and tighten your belt for dear life.

Go ahead and laugh now, but beware: One day, as you stand in front of the mirror, distracted by the inexplicably long hairs that are growing from your nostrils, your mild alarm will turn to sheer terror as your fancy low-riding pants fall down around your ankles.

Q Why are salaries a taboo topic?

A Everybody, it seems, wants to tell all. Don't believe us? Just turn on the TV news; most nights you'll see people whose lives have recently been rocked by personal tragedy but who nonetheless have time to pour their hearts out to anybody brandishing a camera, a microphone, and an expensive haircut. At the bookstore, you'll find stacks of magazines and memoirs that are filled with stories related by famous and not-so-famous people who want to tell us way more about themselves than we need to know—who they slept with, what they snorted. The Internet is teeming with blogs in which people from all walks of life tell us the mundane details of their existences.

But getting people to talk about their salaries? Well, that's not so easy.

According to Ed Lawler, a business professor at the University of Southern California, talking about how much money you earn can make you appear uncouth. "It's a very American, very middle-class phenomenon," Lawler told the *New York Times*. "The way we were raised is that it was bad taste to talk about how much you make." Lawler, who studies salary secrecy, says that many people see no constructive purpose in revealing their salaries. Why? Depending on how much money the other people in the conversation earn, the information can make the blabber-mouth look like a braggart or a loser.

Who really stands to gain from this secrecy? Lawler and others who study the issue agree: employers. Knowledge is power. The less we know about how much our coworkers are getting paid, the easier it is for employers to keep our salaries down. This is one reason why some companies reprimand their employees for discussing their compensation. Lawler has conducted multiple studies that have found that people tend to overestimate how much their coworkers get paid. They assume that their lower sala-ries are the exception and that most other people get paid more. If they only knew.

But it appears that more and more that younger people do know. A study conducted in 2007 for *Money* magazine discovered that people under the age of thirty-five are more willing to discuss their salaries with coworkers. Having grown up as the Internet was exploding onto the scene, they seem more comfortable than their elders with the dissemination of any and all personal information. The ease of Internet anonymity has given rise to a slew of sites where people report their occupations and the wages they earn, allowing others to compile ballpark salary figures for job hunters to use.

The same people who enjoy embarrassing themselves on Twitter and Facebook also have fewer qualms about the traditional social constraints with regard to talking about money. And in the long run, that may pay off for them.

Q Why do people sing in the shower?

A At recording studios, engineers spend thousands of dollars on acoustic foam, ceiling tiles, and other sound-deadening equipment in an attempt to remove as much echo from the room as possible. And sometimes it's all for naught. When the latest scantily clad pop sensation shows up to record an album, the engineers might find themselves electronically goosing the tracks with echo effects, augmenting a voice that is a little less robust than the adoring public might guess.

They could've saved all that money and just recorded the song in the bathroom. With its close quarters and hard, smooth surfaces, the bathroom acts as an echo chamber—sounds are sustained a little longer than normal as they bounce freely around the room. People who are already in love with the sounds of their own voices (you know who you are) find that the echoes make their singing seem fuller and more resonant.

This brand of vanity-enhanced vanity is apparently an international phenomenon. In 2007 a television network in India began producing an amateur talent show called *Bathroom Singer,* in which contestants sang in a bathroom stage setting for cash prizes. Those who didn't show enough *jhaag* (it sounds dirty, but it really just refers to being entertaining) were rudely eliminated from the competition with the sound of a toilet flush.

Q Do countries get paid for delivering mail from other countries?

A Yes, but fortunately, countries work out the tab amongst themselves. Imagine having to buy stamps from every country that handled your letter as it went around the world. This is how people did it in the early days of mail, and it was a real pain.

In 1874, a bunch of nations got together and formed an international organization to sort it all out. The goals were to eliminate the need for countries to establish individual postal treaties with one another and to allow people to buy stamps from whatever country they were in. The organization is now a United Nations agency called the Universal Postal Union (UPO).

Over the years, the UPO has adjusted its formula to make certain that every country receives a fair share of the dough. Initially, the UPO assumed that almost every letter would get a reply, meaning that any two countries would spend about the same amount of time and money delivering mail from the other. As a result, participating countries kept all the money for mail leaving their shores. But with the rise of magazine delivery, mail-order business, and the like, some countries (including the United States) ended up getting the short end of the stick, receiving more mail than they sent. So the UPO instituted terminal dues: payments from the country of origin to the destination country to cover the costs associated with foreign mail.

Today, terminal dues are based on a complex formula that factors in the total weight of the mail and the total number of pieces going from one nation to another, as well as the quality of service in the destination country. For industrialized countries, the formula takes into account the cost of delivering mail in the destination country. For developing countries, the formula uses an average world rate instead of an individual rate.

The math is complicated, and the UPO seems to be forever tweaking its formula. Just be glad the United Nations figures it all out so that you don't have to.

Q Why is it a compliment to be called "as cute as a button"?

A When we say that someone is as cute as a button, what we mean is that he or she is good-looking, but in a unique way. We use the phrase to describe babies, children, and beloved pets because it suggests the type of charm that's the special property of the tiny and defenseless. When something is as cute as a button, you feel the need to take it home so that you can nurture and protect it.

Right now, you're probably wondering: What in the world does that have to do with buttons? Sure, buttons are important—keeping our pants around our waists is just one of their many underrated accomplishments. Even so, you wouldn't call buttons "cute," would you?

According to slang lexicographer Stuart Berg Flexner, the phrase "cute as a button" goes back to 1946. Flexner writes that "cute" was one of "the most overused slang words of the late 1920s and 1930s." And "cute as a button" is just one of many comparative variations on the theme; others include "cute as a bug in a rug" and "cute as a bug's ear." They all describe something that's charming because of its diminutive size or stature.

Interestingly enough, "cute" hasn't always been a compliment. The word entered the English language in the early eighteenth century as a shortened form of "acute," describing someone who is crafty or cunning. You wouldn't compare a schemer like that to a button—but you might say he was "cute as a weasel."

James Joyce used the word in that sense in *Ulysses*, perhaps the most critically lauded novel of the twentieth century. But the phrase he chose was a bit off-color. Joyce, who elsewhere in this eight-hundred-page doorstop broke ground as the first novelist to write an evocative description of a bowel movement, stated that a particularly conniving character is "as cute as an outhouse rat"—except he doesn't say "outhouse."

Yikes! If that's the alternative, we'll take buttons.

Q If New Hampshire is in the USA, where's Old Hampshire?

A In 1622, colonial entrepreneurs Captain John Mason and Sir Ferdinando Gorges received a land grant from the Council for New England for all the territory between the Merrimack and Kennebec rivers. In 1629, the two men split the grant, with Mason's share covering the land south of the Piscataqua River.

Mason named his area New Hampshire, after the English county of Hampshire, a place where he had spent much of his youth. And compared with New Hampshire, the original Hampshire is indeed old. Located on the south coast of England, it was first settled in Neolithic, or early prehistoric, times. Today, Hampshire is bordered by the counties of Wiltshire and Dorset to the west, Berkshire to the north, and West Sussex and Surrey to the east. The county's southern coastline is bounded by the Solent, a strait of the English Channel whose coast is renowned for historic castles, unspoiled nature preserves, and chichi yachting.

Hampshire, about an hour from London by car, is among the largest nonmetropolitan counties, or shires, in England. If you go to "Old Hampshire," be sure to pay your respects to one of its natives, novelist Jane Austen. Her tomb is at Winchester Cathedral.

Q Why do doctors have such lousy handwriting?

A An estimated seven thousand Americans die each year due to incorrect medication or dosages brought about by doctors' sloppy handwriting on prescriptions. Why can't well-educated, literate, responsible, confident medical professionals write legibly? Because doctors are likely to be men—and men in executive positions have lousy handwriting. That's according to a study posted on bmj.com, an online medical journal. It turns out that doctors' handwriting is no worse than that of their peers in other important professions.

Why are doctors singled out? Because what they write—it can be a life-saving prescription—is in a sense powerful and magical. So are doctors themselves, with their special knowledge and exalted position. In this context, their chicken scratches seem oddly infantile and out-of-sync with their training and standing. It's made worse, experts agree, by the arcane symbols that doctors have long used to indicate dosages and schedules, and now by the huge array of drugs with similar-looking names that are easily confused on a sloppily written prescription.

There has been a movement for years to implement prescription-writing computer software that transmits letter-perfect scrips to pharmacies. But this has been slow in coming. Critics argue that it's just as easy to choose the wrong drug on a drop-down menu as it is to write "Celebrex" so illegibly that a busy pharmacist sees "Cialis," and some poor dude's muscles don't get relaxed at all.

Here's some sound advice: Look at your prescription and ask your doctor to repeat it to you. Then make sure your pharmacist understands it the same way. If there's a discrepancy, alert your pharmacist to call your doctor. Your life may depend on it.

CONTRIBUTORS

Tom Harris is a Web project consultant, editor, and writer living in Atlanta. He is the co-founder of Explainist.com, and was leader of the editorial content team at HowStuffWorks.com.

Anthony G. Craine is a contributor to the *Britannica Book of the Year* and has written for magazines including *Inside Sports* and *Ask*. He is a former United Press International bureau chief.

Diane Lanzillotta Bobis is a food, fashion, and lifestyle writer from Glenview, Illinois.

Pat Sherman is a writer living in Cambridge, Massachusetts. She is the author several books for children, including *The Sun's Daughter* and *Ben and the Proclamation of Emancipation*.

Jack Greer is a writer living in Chicago.

Noah Liberman is a Chicago-based sports, entertainment, and business writer who has published two books and has contributed articles to a wide range of newspapers and national magazines.

Joshua D. Boeringa is a writer living in Mt. Pleasant, Michigan. He has written for magazines and Web sites.

Vickey Kalambakal is a writer and historian based in Southern California. She writes for textbooks, encyclopedias, magazines, and ezines.

Alex Nechas is a writer and editor living in Chicago.

Carrie Williford is a writer living in Atlanta. She was a contributing writer to HowStuffWorks.com.

Shanna Freeman is a writer and editor living near Atlanta. She also works in an academic library.

Brett Kyle is a writer living in Draycott, Somerset, England. He also is an actor, musician, singer, and playwright.

Chuck Giametta is a highly acclaimed journalist who specializes in coverage of the automotive industry. He has written and edited books, magazines, and Web articles on many automotive topics.

Jessica Royer Ocken is a freelance writer and editor based in Chicago.

Jeff Moores is an illustrator whose work appears in periodicals and advertisements, and as licensed characters on clothing. Visit his Web site (jeffmoores.com) to see more of his work.

Factual verification: Darcy Chadwick, Barbara Cross, Bonny M. Davidson, Andrew Garrett, Cindy Hangartner, Brenda McLean, Carl Miller, Katrina O'Brien, Marilyn Perlberg